English: An Integrated Course

Books by the same author (published by Hodder and Stoughton)

Directed Writing and Reading
Living English
Drama and Theatre Arts
Don't Guess: an Introduction to Objective Tests in English
Ten Ghost Stories (Ed.)
Ten Science Fiction Stories (Ed.)
Summary and Directed Writing (with F. D. A. Burns)
Advanced English Language (with F. D. A. Burns)
Objective Tests in English Language for GCE (with Brian Rowe)
New Objective Tests in English Language (with Brian Rowe)
Twenty Summaries in English Language (with Brian Rowe)

English: An Integrated Course

A Unit based approach to GCSE

R. A. Banks, MA, PhD

HODDER AND STOUGHTON

LONDON   SYDNEY   AUCKLAND   TORONTO

ISBN 0 340 38991 5

First published 1986

Printed in Great Britain
for Hodder and Stoughton Educational
a division of Hodder and Stoughton Ltd, Mill Road
Dunton Green, Sevenoaks, Kent by
The Eastern Press Ltd., London and Reading.

For: Mary-Lou

ACKNOWLEDGMENTS

The author and publisher would like to thank the following for permission to reproduce copyright work in this book: Her Majesty's Stationery Office for an extract from the National Criteria for English; Faber and Faber Ltd for an extract from *The Lord of the Flies* by William Golding; The Society of Authors on behalf of the Bernard Shaw estate for one extract ('The Golden Rule') from *Man and Superman* by Bernard Shaw; Laurence Pollinger Ltd for 'The Case for the Defence' from *Collected Stories* by Graham Greene published by William Heinemann Ltd and The Bodley Head Ltd; David Higham Associates Ltd for 'To a Conscript of 1940' from *Selected Poems* by Sir Herbert Read; George Sassoon for 'A Case for the Miners' by Siegfried Sassoon; Vallentine Mitchell & Co. Ltd for an extract from *The Diary of Anne Frank*; Methuen London for six extracts from *The Secret Diary of Adrian Mole, aged 13¾* by Sue Townsend; Vallentine Mitchell & Co. Ltd for an extract from *Ash on a Young Man's Sleeve* by Dannie Abse; Chatto & Windus for extracts from *Cider With Rosie* by Laurie Lee; Faber & Faber Ltd for 'Love', an uncollected verse (first published in the *Critical Quarterly*, Summer 1966) by Philip Larkin; The Literary Executors of the Estate of H. G. Wells and William Heinemann Ltd for an extract from *The Time Machine* by H. G. Wells; William Heinemann Ltd and Little, Brown & Co. for an extract from *Dear Me* by Peter Ustinov; 'Child Half Asleep' by Tony Connor from *New and Selected Poems*, published in Great Britain by Anvil Press Poetry Ltd, and in the United States by the University of Georgia Press © 1982 The University of Georgia Press; David Higham Associates Ltd for an extract from *Quite Early One Morning* by Dylan Thomas, published by J. M. Dent; Hodder & Stoughton for an extract from *The Encyclopaedia of Dates and Events* by Jenkins, Lee and Pascoe; Octopus Books for four extracts from *The World's Greatest Cranks and Crackpots* by M. Nicholas; The University of London School Examining Board for extracts from opening scenes in O level papers (January 1981, January 1980, January 1979, January 1985 and June 1978) by R. A. Banks; Anthony Sheil Associates Ltd and Hutchinson Books Ltd for 'The Trial' from *The Gallows Tree* by Dannie Abse; Penguin Books Ltd for an extract from 'My Apprenticeship' by Maxim Gorky, translated by Ronald Wilks © Ronald Wilks 1974; Faber & Faber Ltd for 'Toads Revisited' from *The Whitsun Weddings* by Philip Larkin; The Marvell Press, England for 'Toads' from *The Less Deceived* by Philip Larkin; Faber & Faber Ltd for 'Bagpipe Music' from *The Collected Poems of Louis MacNiece*; Edward Blishen for three extracts from *The Roaring Boys* by Edward Blishen, first published by Thames and Hudson; Michael Joseph Ltd in association with M. and J. Hobbs for 'Soldier Freddy' by Spike Milligan; Curtis Brown, London for 'Lather as you Go' © Ogden Nash 1951, 'What's the Use', 'England Expects' and 'Children's Party' by Ogden Nash; Putnam & Co. Ltd for 'The Anatomy of Humour' by Morris Bishop © Morris Bishop and Putnam & Co.; John Murray (Publishers) Ltd for 'Harvest Hymn' from *Collected Poems* by John Betjeman; John Cape Ltd for an extract from 'Chips with Everything' by Arnold Wesker; William Morris Agency (UK) Ltd for an extract from *Another Stretch of Porridge* by Dick Clement and Ian la Frenais; Octopus Books Ltd for five extracts from *Strange But True*, edited by T. Healey; A. D. Peters & Co. Ltd for an extract from *Thus I Refute Beelzy* by John Collier; Edward Arnold (Publishers) Ltd for 'Tender-Heartedness' by Harry Graham from *Ruthless Rhymes for Heartless Homes*; George Allen & Unwin for 'Schoolboy' from *Little Johnny's Confessions* by Brian Patten; Faber & Faber Ltd for 'My parents kept me from children who were rough' by Stephen Spender from *Collected Poems*; David Higham Associates Ltd for an extract from *Portrait of the Artist as a Young Dog* by Dylan Thomas, published by J. M. Dent; Penguin Books Ltd for an extract from 'Zigger Zagger' from *Zigger Zagger/Mooney and his Caravans* by Peter Terson © Peter Terson 1970; David Higham Associates Ltd for 'My Grandmother' from *Collected Poems* by Elizabeth Jennings published by Macmillan; Faber & Faber Ltd for 'The Garden' by Ezra Pound from *Collected Shorter Poems*; Octopus Books Ltd for two extracts and one adaptation of an extract from *The World's Worst Disasters*; David Higham Associates Ltd for 'History of the Flood' by John Heath-Stubbs published by Oxford University Press; James Kirkup for 'Undivided Loyalty', 'Rugby League Game' and 'Tea in a Spaceship' from *The Prodigal Son* first published by Oxford University Press; Routledge & Kegan Paul plc for 'Death of a Son' from *Selected Poems* by Jon Silkin; Her Majesty's Stationery Office for an extract from *The Bullock Report*; Laurence Pollinger Ltd and the Estate of Richard Church for an extract from *Over the Bridge* by Richard Church; Doubleday & Co. Inc. for 'The fun they had' from *Earth is Room Enough* by Isaac Asimov; Newnes Books for two tables from *A Survey of Rewards and Punishments* by M. E. Highfield and A. Pinsent; Francisco Campbell Custodio and Ad. Donker (Pty) Ltd for 'Horses on the Camargue' by Roy Campbell; the Executors of the Estate of C. Day Lewis and Jonathan Cape Ltd for 'Two Travellers' from *Collected Poems 1954* by C. Day Lewis published by Jonathan Cape Ltd and Hogarth Press; David Higham Associates Ltd for the conclusion to 'Expedition to Earth' from *The Best of Arthur C. Clarke 1937–71* published by Gollancz; Faber & Faber Ltd for 'Dawn Shoot' from *Death of a Naturalist* by Seamus Heaney; Times Newspapers Ltd for the article '41 Soccer Fans die in Stampede at Euro Cup Final' by David Miller (*The Times* 30.5.85).

We have made every effort to trace owners of copyright material reproduced in this book and would be grateful for any information leading to copyright holders of texts not acknowledged above.

The author and publisher would also like to thank the following for permission to reproduce photographs in this book: John Hillelson Agency Ltd for the photo on page 28; The Imperial War Museum for the photos on pages 47 and 131; Times Newspapers Ltd for 'Olympic city then and now' on page 64 (*Sunday Times Colour Supplement* 27.5.84) and for 'Jobless queue growth declining' by David Smith on page 77 (*The Times* 3.8.85); Southampton Art Gallery and Museums for 'Work' by David Redfern on page 81; The Bridgeman Art Library for 'Dismayed Artist' by Frederick Daniel Hardy (Wolverhampton Central Art Gallery) on page 82; Chris Jones for the photo on page 120; Roger Viollet for the photo on page 121; Punch for the two cartoons on pages 93 and 94; the Vienna Kunsthistorisches Museum for 'Kinderspiele' ('Children's Games') by P. Breugel the Elder on page 120; the British Museum for 'Spring cleaning in Noah's Ark' by W. Heath-Robinson on page 126; Topham Picture Library for the photos on pages 133, 134 and 159; Kids International Ltd for the photos on pages 150–151 and the National Film Archive for the stills from *Lord of the Flies* (page 15), *Blue Lagoon* (page 29), *Les Dernières Vacances* (page 39), *The Time Machine* (page 41), *American Werewolf in London* (page 55), *Metropolis* (page 69), *Big Business* (page 83), *Psycho* (page 97), *Feet First* (page 111), *Towering Inferno* (page 123), *Belles of St Trinians* (page 139), *Star Trek* (page 153) and *Rocky* (page 165).

CONTENTS

INTRODUCTION

This book is intended to do two things: first, to help teachers and pupils understand what is required of them in English in the GCSE examination and, secondly, to provide a store of integrated material on which to work, varied in its content and of the right kind likely to appeal to pupils at all levels of ability.

The GCSE is not a mere bringing-together of former CSE and GCE syllabuses. The working groups responsible for devising the new examination set about producing new approaches that would appeal to the majority of students in the final stages of their secondary courses at 16+ and that would allow the best that they could achieve to be assessed. Five area boards were set up to administer the GCSE in England and Wales: the Southern Examining Group (SEG), the Midland Examining Group (MEG), the Northern Examining Association (NEA), the London East-Anglian Group (LEAG), and the Welsh Examining Board (WEB); Scotland, of course, has already begun its own system of examining achievement at 16+ following the Munn-Dunning Report. The syllabuses and schemes of assessment in English vary from examining group to examining group but they all nevertheless have writing, understanding and expression, summary, and an oral element, to name but a few. For school candidates course-work will play some part in the assessment (a minimum of 20% normally) and most schemes will allow a combination of course-work and assessment by final examination. This book discusses in some detail what is expected from the students, especially in course-work and in oral English (both listening and talking) and offers a wide variety of material they can use to achieve their goals.

The part of the book which provides work material for GCSE candidates is arranged in integrated course units. Already some syllabuses in schools have begun to be broken down into such units but it is not suggested by any means that all English Departments will wish to restrict themselves to such 'units'. The material in this book is grouped under such headings as *Falling In and Out of Love*, *Humour*, *Time Warps*, *Work: Becoming A Sorcerer's Apprentice* as a way of focussing attention over a short period on some interesting, well-written examples of prose, poetry, drama, journalism, and other media forms of expression from which individual and class-work programmes can spring. These areas are integrated with oral work; the material runs across the curriculum but it is based largely on the twentieth century and is likely to appeal to the full ability range. At the same time there are enough backward glances to earlier periods to allow teachers and students to explore together work by writers such as Shakespeare, Marlowe, Pepys, Emily Brontë, and Lewis Carroll; there are even humorous extracts in translation from the Anglo-Saxons and the Vikings. Above all the aim has been to provide lively, well-integrated, accessible examples of past and present English for further exploration. Students can use the book on their own. Resourceful teachers will be able to adapt and extend its material to form a successful basis for GCSE work.

Finally, I am again indebted to my wife, Mary-Lou, for her patience and care; she read the manuscript as it was being produced and offered valuable criticism and suggestions to supplement those by other practising teachers. Mrs Daphne Meeking once again prepared an immaculate typescript with her usual good humour, attention to detail, and immense professional skill. Without them the final work would have been much more difficult to produce.

R.A.B.
Sunbury-on-Thames
1986

PREFACE

What are you expected to be able to do in English?

Some attempt has been made by those responsible for designing the new GCSE to describe this.

First, *your course should have helped you to develop the ability to:*
– communicate accurately, appropriately, and effectively in writing;
– understand and respond imaginatively to what you hear, read, and experience in a variety of media;
– enjoy and appreciate the reading of literature;
– understand yourself and others.

Secondly, *it should have given you ample opportunity to show that you can*:
– understand and convey information;
– understand, order and present facts, ideas, and opinions;
– evaluate information in reading material and in other media, and select what is relevant to specific purposes;
– articulate experience and express what is felt and what is imagined;
– recognise implicit meaning and attitudes;
– show a sense of audience and an awareness of style in both formal and informal situations;
– exercise control of appropriate grammatical structures, conventions of paragraphing, sentence structure, punctuation and spelling in your writing;
– communicate effectively and appropriately in spoken English.

(National Criteria for English)

The emphasis, then, is on **understanding** what you read and hear, **responding** to it, and **expressing** your thoughts and feelings **appropriately** and **effectively** with due regard paid to *grammar*, *punctuation*, and *spelling*. All these skills are interrelated and will be assessed from your work as a whole.

How can you show your ability?

There are a number of ways that have been devised to help you:
I   course-work, some of which is done in class and some at home;
II   examinations and by tests;
III   talking individually and in groups.

Some schemes put a lot of emphasis on course-work and some on examinations but all schemes for school candidates at least, must include at least a fifth of the assessment based on course-work and all schemes must include an assessment of your ability in Spoken English.

PART ONE

I. Course-work

The course-work folder you offer for assessment should comprise a selection of the best work you have done during your period of preparation for the GCSE assessment. Some of the work may consist of units related to each other but some should consist of single, self-contained, continuous pieces of writing.

Normally about *five or six pieces of work* are required if 50% of your final assessment is by course-work and about *ten to twelve pieces* if your final assessment is totally by course-work. Each piece should be long enough to show what you can do to the best of your ability and some of the boards responsible for the final award suggest that it should be about 400-500 words in length.

One or two pieces may have to be done in what are described as 'controlled' conditions in the classroom: that is, you will be expected to write for about an hour on a topic you have already had an opportunity to think about, but for most of the pieces you will have had ample opportunity to draft and re-draft, although if you do extensive re-drafting you will be expected to submit your earlier versions as well as your last in order to show what changes you have made.

The pieces of work you include in your folder should cover a range of material on which you have worked during your course in order to show your ability in many fields in English. Some of the areas you might like to consider are:

(i)   personal writing;
(ii)   descriptive writing, including explanations of how problems might be solved or tasks performed;
(iii)   narrative writing;
(iv)   writing to demonstrate discussion or argument;
(v)   writing to demonstrate your ability to explain;
(vi)   writing about a book or books you have enjoyed;
(vii)   writing which explores themes or ideas taken from what you have studied and enjoyed both in English and in other subjects.
(viii) work on drama and the theatre;
(xi)   work on media and other forms of communication in English such as newspapers, magazines and advertising material;
(x)   writing which shows your ability to read or to listen carefully and your understanding;
(xi)   work involving the selection of ideas from passages, books, graphs, diagrams, computer material, and the re-arranging and re-presenting of the ideas for another purpose and for another audience – in order words, work which allows you to show skill in both **summary and directed writing;**
(xii)   writing which shows your ability to respond to stimuli such as pictures, music, films, sculpture, architecture and other experiences which move

you imaginatively, emotionally, and in your thoughts to talk and write about them.

These twelve suggested areas are not those specifically required by GCSE boards but they do represent comprehensively the kind of writing which might usefully be included in a course-work folder. Later in this book suggested 'units' of work in English will allow you to explore all these kinds in a variety of ways.

All the GCSE boards will expect your work to be as accurately written as you can possibly make it. With the pieces of course-work which you have an opportunity to re-draft and to revise, you should be able to check them through carefully to make sure that you have used sentences properly, that your paragraph structures are appropriate, that you have followed the conventions of spelling, that you have used punctuation carefully to reflect the meaning you want to convey clearly to your reader, and that you have borne in mind the four essential features of all good writing and speaking:

(*i*)   a clear point of view;
(*ii*) a well-structured 'message';
(*iii*) an awareness of what is appropriate to the context in which you are using English;
(*iv*) a sense of 'audience' or 'reader'.

You will find in the 'units' later in this book many suggestions to help you take account of these matters in your writing. After all, a GCSE award in English is intended to reflect and to indicate to others your ability to use the language effectively and appropriately.

Finally, take a pride in the way you present your folder of work for assessment. Your teacher will advise you how to select and assemble the material to include in it; but remember that it is intended to represent the very best that you can do across the wide range of skills in language and literature that make up the subject of English.

How will your course-work be assessed

Already the qualities looked for in your work have been briefly described.

Normally your own class teacher or tutor will assess your work. It should carry your name and the date on which you submit it for assessment, although if you have worked on it over a period of time and re-drafted it on one or more occasions the dates on which the stages of a long piece of work were handed in ought to be shown. The work you submit for assessment must be in its final form: that is, all the revisions you want to make must have been completed. Any alterations you have made to an earlier piece of work must be made clear; this is normally done by attaching the original piece of writing, with any comments on it, to your final one.

Once you have selected **the appropriate range** and number of pieces of work which reveal your real abilities you should gather them together to form a folder. The folder's first page should list the work it contains and all the pages should be tagged together. In most GCSE course-work folders this first page should also declare formally that all the writing is your own and not copied from other sources of any kind. All the pieces should be written by hand and not typed, although pictures, charts and diagrams you need to support your work may be photocopied provided you acknowledge where you got them from.

The teacher assessing the folder (sometimes called the 'teacher assessor') will be required normally to mark the folder *as a whole,* rather than to add up the marks or grades for the individual pieces and then average them out. It is the picture of the candidate's ability in English across a range of different kinds of writing and of different forms (plays, diaries, formal and informal letters, summaries, reports, etc.) that is to be assessed for the final award.

Someone in the centre or school where the candidates are working will be responsible for ensuring that the work of all the candidates is assessed reliably in accordance with the standards laid down by the GCSE boards, that the assessments are valid, and that common marking procedures and standards have been applied to all the classes, sets or streams in the centre. To make sure that all the assessments are based on comparable standards, the teachers who are responsible for the initial marking of candidates' work in a particular centre will normally attend trials, sometimes called 'internal conformity trials' which aim to ensure that one teacher's standards of marking conform to those of another. It is important that every centre should establish that all the marking has been done in accordance with the standards of assessment laid down and later moderated by the GCSE boards.

The next stage in the assessment is that of ensuring that the standards have been maintained from one centre or school to another. This work is carried out in area groupings, sometimes called 'area consortia'. Marks awarded by teacher assessors will be sent to an area moderator or a review panel responsible for checking the standards of marking by examining a number of folders reflecting the whole ability range of candidates, at a particular centre. The moderator's or review panel's job is to ensure that the proper standards have been applied to the assessment; if necessary, more examples of folders or, indeed, *all* the folders from one centre can be called for if necessary. It is also a moderator's task to arrange 'agreement-trial' meetings for teacher assessors before the final work of assessment even begins; at these 'agreement-trial' meetings examples of work at every level of performance will be discussed and the standards of marking will be established.

Later, the marks that have been scrutinised by moderators will then be submitted to district examiners or chief examiners who, with the GCSE board, will make the final awards.

This lengthy procedure is followed so that the results can be seen to be *reliable* and *valid* and *comparable* between one centre's candidates and another's.

The procedures vary in detail from one GCSE board to another, of course, but they are all aimed to ensure consistency and co-ordination in assessing work.

II. Examinations

All the GCSE boards offer at least one scheme of assessment where it is possible to combine both an externally set and assessed examination and a course-work folder. Often the proportion of examination to course work can be varied to emphasise one rather than the other. Where the two forms of assessment are combined, however, course work must account for at least 20% of the total marks.

The form and content of the examination differ from board to board and depend on the proportion of course work with which it is to be assessed. An example will illustrate the point; syllabuses may, of course, be amended from time to time. The 100% assessment by examination is usually restricted to those candidates (e.g. overseas or in Further/Adult education) where centres would find course work difficult to assess and moderate.

e.g.: The London East-Anglian Group

50% Final External Examination

2 hours. Related passages of various kinds for commentary and directed writing to demonstrate detailed reading and handling material for specific purposes.

The tests may require an understanding of instructions presented in a variety of ways and contexts, the location and selection of information relevant to particular topics, the selecting (and re-ordering where appropriate) of given information for specific purposes and audiences. Candidates should expect, too, to identify the purposes and contexts of different kinds of written communications and to be able to detect pre-suppositions, implications, assumptions, irrelevance and illogicality in different kinds of material. They may be asked to demonstrate their ability to recognise and evaluate consistency and coherence in various kinds of written communication which they should be able to evaluate for mood, attitude and bias. Their written work should take note of the effect on meaning of such aspects as form, structure and organisation, pace and contrast, phrasing and idiom, and figurative language. They will also be assessed on their ability to read both literary and non-literary material with close attention to detail, to handle ideas for a specific purpose, and to express themselves appropriately and accurately. They may be asked to write logically or persuasively, to convey an attitude or a mood (for example, embarrassment, confidence, sadness), to slant material, or to aim at evoking a specific response from particular readers.

III. Oral English

The National Criteria for English make it clear from the outset that skills in English are interrelated and interdependent. One of the skills which they list in their objectives for candidates taking GCSE assessments is that of being able to 'communicate effectively and appropriately in spoken English', (2.1.8). Later the paper setting out the English criteria becomes more specific:

> The interactive nature of listening and speaking cannot be demonstrated solely by reading aloud or delivering a talk. Reading aloud can be an appropriate way of demonstrating some aspects of reading comprehension and the preparation of a talk can involve valuable reading and writing skills. They have, therefore, a useful role to play in the assessment of the spoken language by providing useful contexts for the interview and/or discussion in which both listening and speaking are to be assessed.
> Conversation and discussion have varying degrees of formality from chat to interview and debate, but for assessment purposes there must be some aim or goal, not simply a random exchange of views. There can be problems in group discussion of assessing the individual performance and response; an individual conversation can help to verify the assessments. (5.2).

Later in the same document the standards or criteria set out for the awards of particular grades in Oral English are given and a close consideration of them will show the areas which you should concentrate on:

Grade 4
The candidate can be expected to have demonstrated competence in:
– understanding and conveying straightforward information;
– presenting facts, ideas, and opinions in orderly sequence;
– selecting and commenting on spoken and written material with sense of relevance;
– describing experience in simple terms and expressing intelligently what is felt and what is imagined;
– recognising statements of opinion and attitude;
– using some variation in speech style according to situation and audience;
– speaking audibily and intelligibly with some sense of appropriate tone, intonation, and pace.

Grade 2
The candidate can be expected to have demonstrated competence in:
– understanding and conveying both straightforward and more complex information;
– ordering and presenting facts, ideas and opinions with a degree of clarity and accuracy;
– evaluating spoken and written material and highlighting what is relevant for specific purposes;
– describing and reflecting upon experience and expressing effectively what is felt and what is imagined;
– recognising statements of opinion and attitude and discerning underlying assumptions and points of view;

– showing sensitivity in using a range of speech styles appropriate to situation and audience;

– speaking clearly and coherently with appropriate tone, intonation, and pace.

A comparison of these two sets of criteria (or statements of how your work will be assessed) should allow you to see how the award of the higher grade depends on greater detail, better ordering of what you say, accuracy and relevance, being able to reflect on what you are saying and seeing the implicit and underlying assumptions in what other people are saying, a high degree of sensitivity to what is appropriate to the context and the audience, and clarity and coherence.

Oral work will usually be assessed by means of collaborative talk and may take a number of different forms in group work: e.g. formal and informal discussions stimulated by different media including literary and non-literary texts, film, television, radio, and visual material; talks given to large and small groups; role-play exercises and simulation games which encourage the exploration of different language styles; scripted drama and improvisation; interviews; and the reading aloud of passages of prose and verse.

In preparing for your assessement in Oral English you might like to bear in mind some of the following aspects of the spoken language as it is used:

– speakers often use different accents, dialogues, and grammatical structures to make their points;

– listening is often an important prerequisite to talking;

– tone of voice, loudness or softness, pace and rhythm are accompanying features to the words themselves and affect meaning and may well affect a listener's reaction;

– eye contact (looking directly at the person to whom you are talking or looking aside), gesture, pausing, and timing will be part of the meaning of what you are saying;

– what is appropriate to one audience or set of circumstances may not be appropriate to another.

One GCSE group specifies very clearly that oral English will be assessed on content, interpersonal skills, language style and structure, and clarity of expression. For **content** candidates will be assessed on the selection, organisation, development, and relevance of what they say. For **interpersonal skills** they will be assessed on their awareness of the audience or listener to whom they are speaking, their ability to listen sensitively, to respond to initiatives taken by others in discussion, to sustain collaborative talk, and to be conscious of the particular context in which the speech activity is taking place. These skills involve, of course, the readiness to tolerate and to follow the expression of an opinion which they do not necessarily hold themselves, the effective use of specifically and carefully framed questions, and an awareness of the non-verbal skills used in dialogue, conversation, or discussion. For **language style and structure** candidates need to be aware of some of the basic differences between spoken and written English grammar, vocabulary, and syntax and to be able to demonstrate their ability to adapt to the range of differing language styles used appropriate to specific contexts. For **clarity of expression** candidates should be able to speak audibly and clearly with some range of pitch and emphasis, although the speech might occasionally be hesitant and uneven; even the best speakers rephrase their ideas, search for words, and modify earlier statements as they go along. Ability here should not be confused with glib fluency.

PART TWO: INTEGRATED WORK UNITS

The *Preface* and *Part One* of this book have set out in some detail what will be expected of successful candidates in GCSE assessments.

Part Two offers units of work, any one of which might form the basis of GCSE work in English over half a term during the eighteen months or two years before the final assessment. The units are not intended to be sequential in any way or to be 'staged' in difficulty from one to the next. Neither need all the suggestions in any single unit be followed up. It is for the teacher and the pupil to decide the best way to use the material in the units, but they are intended to provide appropriate and integrated English work in context for those preparing for either course-work or final examination assessments or a combination of both in written and spoken English, linked with literature, media studies, drama, or other areas of the curriculum embraced by the study of English.

The material provided brings together writing, reading, comprehension, summary, oral work and all the other English skills in an *integrated* way. Students should bear in mind that no skill in English exists in isolation; English requires a context in which it is used and the most careful student takes account of this context to use the language, whether written or spoken, **appropriately.**

Unit 1

Changing things: a new society

If you and your friends suddenly found yourselves deposited on an island, with everything you needed to keep yourselves alive, you would have the chance to set up your own society from scratch, without the interference of 'authority'; you would have to set up your own rules and punishments, your own organisations to make sure that everyone's 'rights' were respected and that everyone contributed to the good of everybody else, and your own ways of living together.

The idea of breaking away into a new world with a chance of fresh beginnings is one that many writers have used as a way of thinking about what is really important in society: from Ulysses in Greek times to Sir Thomas More (*Utopia*) during Henry the Eighth's reign, to Jonathan Swift (*Gulliver's Travels*) in 1762, to George Orwell (*Animal Farm*) at the end of the Second World War, to Arthur C. Clarke's *2001: A Space Odyssey* in 1968, to mention but a few examples.

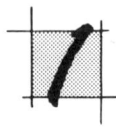

Following an atomic explosion a group of children have been evacuated in an aeroplane carrying its own detachable passenger tube. In the tropics the plane is attacked by the enemy but manages to drop its tube full of children on an island before flying off in flames out to sea. The tube crash-lands and most of its occupants survive the disaster. This is the background to William Golding's *Lord of the Flies* (1954) and at a meeting the children decide what to do next:

Ralph cleared his throat.

'Well then.'

All at once he found he could talk fluently and explain what he had to say. He passed a hand through his fair hair and spoke.

'We're on an island. We've been on the mountain-top and seen water all round. We saw no houses, no smoke, no footprints, no boats, no people. We're on an uninhabited island with no other people on it.'

Jack broke in.

'All the same you need an army — for hunting. Hunting pigs —'

'Yes. There are pigs on the island.'

'There aren't any grown-ups. We shall have to look after ourselves.'

The meeting hummed and was silent.

'And another thing. We can't have everybody talking at once. We'll have to have 'Hands up' like at school.'

He held the conch before his face and glanced round the mouth.

'Then I'll give him the conch.'

'Conch?'

'That's what this shell's called. I'll give the conch to the next person to speak. He can hold it when he's speaking.'

'But —'

'Look —'

'And he won't be interrupted. Except by me.'

Jack was on his feet.

'We'll have rules! ' he cried excitedly. 'Lots of rules. Then when anyone breaks 'em —'

'Whee-oh!'

'Wacco!'

'Bong!'

'Doink!'

Ralph felt the conch lifted from his lap. Then Piggy was standing cradling the great cream shell and the shouting died down. Jack, left on his feet, looked uncertainly at Ralph who smiled and patted the log. Jack sat down. Piggy took off his glasses and blinked at the assembly while he wiped them on his shirt.

'You're hindering Ralph. You're not letting him get to the most important thing.'

He paused effectively.

'Who knows we're here? Eh?'

'They knew at the airport.'

'The man with a trumpet-thing —'

'My dad.'

Piggy put on his glasses.

'Nobody knows where we are,' said Piggy. He was paler than before and breathless. 'Perhaps they knew where we was going to; and perhaps not. But they don't know where we are 'cos we never got there.' He gaped at them for a moment, then swayed and sat down. Ralph took the conch from his hands.

'That's what I was going to say,' he went on 'when you all, all... .' He gazed at their intent faces. 'The plane was shot down in flames. Nobody knows where we are. We may be here a long time.'

The silence was so complete that they could hear the fetch and miss of Piggy's breathing. The sun slanted in and lay golden over half the platform. The breezes that on the lagoon had chased their tails like kittens were finding their way across the platform and into the forest. Ralph pushed back the tangle of fair hair that hung on his forehead.

'So we may be here a long time.'

Nobody said anything.

William Golding, *Lord of the Flies*

Leadership

(*a*) Find out what you can about a man or woman who had become a leader of a group of people or even of a nation (e.g. Mrs Indira Gandhi, Hitler, Moses, etc.). What qualities did he or she have to become a leader?

(*b*) Make a list of those things you would expect the leader of a group of children on a desert island (such as that in the extract) to have. Try to explain why each of them is important.

(*c*) Look up the following words in a dictionary and write down the definitions you find for each one:

leader; representative; delegate; spokesman; monarch; dictator; director; captain; president; sultan.

What common elements can you find in the definitions?

(*d*) Now make a list of all those qualities you would expect to find ideally in a leader. (Make it clear from the outset what group of people the leader is leading.)

(*e*) Discuss with others in your own English group how important it is to have leaders at all. What alternatives can you find to the idea of 'a leader'?

Rules

(*a*) Here is a well-known set of ten rules on which many societies, beginning with the early Jews, have been based. They were not an independent code of laws but set out the basic principles on which all of Israel's laws were to be interpreted and applied.

(*i*)   Worship only the one true god.

(*ii*)   Do not make carved images to worship.

(*iii*) Do not abuse God's name.

(*iv*)   Respect the sabbath day.

(*v*)   Honour your mother and father.

(*vi*)   Do not commit murder.

(*vii*) Do not commit adultery.

(*viii*) Do not steal.

(*ix*)   Do not give false evidence against anyone.

(*x*)   Do not covet anyone else's house, wife, or goods.

What other 'codes' of behaviour followed by different peoples can you find? (Explore the rules underlying the ways of life based on Hinduism, or Shintoism, or Sikhism, or Mohammedism, for example.)

In *Man and Superman* (1905) G. B. Shaw gave a new slant to the making of rules:

THE GOLDEN RULE

Do not do unto others as you would they should do unto you. Their tastes may not be the same.

Never resist temptation: prove all things: hold fast that which is good.

Do not love thy neighbour as yourself. If you are on good terms with yourself it is an impertinence: if on bad, an injury.

The golden rule is that there are no golden rules.

(*b*) Make a list of your school or college rules. Then try to justify or defend them.

What would you change?

What would you add to them?

Crime and Punishment

(*a*) Every society has had to try to find ways of dealing with those of its members who failed to follow the rules. Crime is defined in Chambers' *Twentieth-Century Dictionary* as: *a violation of law, especially if serious: an act punishable by law.*

Write down your ideas on some of the following:

Are there any 'laws' of your country which you could ever justify breaking? (Or 'rules' of your school, if you prefer.)

What are the differences between 'criminal law' and 'civil law'? How do you explain the differences? Are they justified?

How is a law made?

Which *one* new law would you like to see introduced? Argue the case for it.

(*b*) In most countries there is some kind of police force whose job it is to enforce the law. Usually it is not their work to decide who is guilty or who is innocent — that is the work of the courts — but clearly in trying to decide whether to prosecute an individual or organisation the police often have to try to interpret laws. This leaves them vulnerable, because the distinction between 'interpretation' and 'enforcement' of law is a fine one.

Investigate one or more of the following topics and then add your own comments to what you find:

(*i*)   How is your local police force organised? (A visit to a police station or a letter to the Chief Constable might help you with your inquiries!)

(*ii*)   What are the advantages and disadvantages of such an organisation of the local police force?

   (*iii*)   What accusations are commonly made against the police? What justification for them can you find? How do the police themselves deal with complaints against them?

   (*iv*)   What alternatives to the idea of a police force can you find? (Consider, for example, the role of a military force, civilian neighbourhood watch schemes, vigilantes, private security organisations, etc.)

(*c*) Arrange to visit the local Magistrate's Court or a higher court of justice. For a visit to the Crown Court you should write to the Chief Clerk of the Court; for a visit to the local Magistrate's Court you should write to the Clerk to the Justices. In both instances you should write well in advance of the visit to seek the court's approval and to confirm that the court will be in session. From the public gallery you will be able to follow the proceedings and listen to cases for the prosecution and defence.

Obtain reports from two different newspapers of a day's proceedings at an important trial or one of immense local interest. Examine them carefully and make lists of similar points given in both and of points which occur in one but not in the other. Then, using the lists, write a brief summary of the day's events from the point of view of either a friendly or hostile witness.

(*d*) Describe your own (or a friend's) personal contacts with the police or encounter with 'the law'. Make it clear how you saw the experience at the time and how you see it now.

(*e*) Courts often have difficulty in interpreting the real truth. Read the following short story and then answer the questions which follow it. It is called 'The Case for the Defence' and is taken from Graham Greene's *Collected Stories*:

It was the strangest murder trial I ever attended. They named it the Peckham murder in the headlines, though Northwood Street, where the old woman was found battered to death, was not strictly speaking in Peckham. This was not one of those cases of circumstantial evidence, in which you feel the
5 jurymen's anxiety — because mistakes *have* been made — like domes of silence muting the court. No, this murderer was all but found with the body; no one present when the Crown counsel outlined his case believed that the man in the dock stood any chance at all.

    He was a heavy stout man with bulging bloodshot eyes. All his muscles
10 seemed to be in his thighs. Yes, an ugly customer, one you wouldn't forget in a hurry — and that was an important point because the Crown proposed to call four witnesses who hadn't forgotten him, who had seen him hurrying away from the little red villa in Northwood Street. The clock had just struck two in the morning.

15   Mrs Salmon in 15 Northwood Street had been unable to sleep; she heard a door click shut and thought it was her own gate. So she went to the window and saw Adams (that was his name) on the steps of Mrs Parker's house. He had just come out and was wearing gloves. He had a hammer in his hand and she saw him drop it into the laurel bushes by the front gate. But before he
20 moved away, he had looked up — at her window. The fatal instinct that tells a man when he is watched exposed him in the light of a street-lamp to her gaze — his eyes suffused with horrifying and brutal fear, like an animal's when you raise a whip. I talked afterwards to Mrs Salmon, who naturally after the

astonishing verdict went in fear herself. As I imagine did all the witnesses—

25 Henry MacDougall, who had been driving home from Benfleet late and nearly ran Adams down at the corner of Northwood Street. Adams was walking in the middle of the road looking dazed. And old Mr Wheeler who lived next door to Mrs Parker, at No. 12, and was wakened by a noise—like a chair falling—through the thin-as-paper villa wall, and got up and looked out

30 of the window, just as Mrs Salmon had done, saw Adams's back and as he turned, those bulging eyes. In Laurel Avenue he had been seen by yet another witness—his luck was badly out; he might as well have committed the crime in broad daylight.

'I understand,' counsel said, 'that the defence proposes to plead mistaken

35 identity. Adams's wife will tell you that he was with her at two in the morning on February 14, but after you have heard the witnesses for the Crown and examined carefully the features of the prisoner, I do not think you will be prepared to admit the possibility of a mistake.'

It was all over, you would have said, but the hanging.

40   After the formal evidence had been given by the policeman who had found the body and the surgeon who examined it, Mrs Salmon was called. She was the ideal witness, with her slight Scotch accent and her expression of honesty, care and kindness.

The counsel for the Crown brought the story gently out. She spoke very

45 firmly. There was no malice in her, and no sense of importance at standing there in the Central Criminal Court with a judge in scarlet hanging on her words and the reporters writing them down. Yes, she said, and then she had gone downstairs and rung up the police station.

'And do you see the man here in court?'

50   She looked straight at the big man in the dock, who stared hard at her with his pekingese eyes without emotion.

'Yes,' she said, 'there he is.'

'You are quite certain?'

She said simply, 'I couldn't be mistaken, sir.'

55   It was all as easy as that.

'Thank you, Mrs Salmon.'

Counsel for the defence rose to cross-examine. If you had reported as many murder trials as I have, you would have known beforehand what line he would take. And I was right, up to a point.

60   'Now, Mrs Salmon, you must remember that a man's life may depend on your evidence.'

'I do remember it, sir.'

'Is your eyesight good?'

'I have never had to wear spectacles, sir.'

65   'You are a woman of fifty-five?'

'Fifty-six, sir.'

'And the man you saw was on the other side of the road?'

'Yes, sir.'

'And it was two o'clock in the morning. You must have remarkable eyes,

70 Mrs Salmon?'

'No, sir. There was moonlight, and when the man looked up, he had the lamplight on his face.'

'And you have no doubt whatever that man you saw is the prisoner?'

I couldn't make out what he was at. He couldn't have expected any other
75 answer than the one he got.

'None whatever, sir. It isn't a face one forgets.'

Counsel took a look round the court for a moment. Then he said, 'Do you
mind, Mrs Salmon, examining again the people in court? No, not the
prisoner. Stand up, please, Mr Adams,' and there at the back of the court, with
80 thick stout body and muscular legs and a pair of bulging eyes, was the exact
image of the man in the dock. He was even dressed the same — tight blue suit
and striped tie.

'Now think very carefully, Mrs Salmon. Can you still swear that the man you
saw drop the hammer in Mrs Parker's garden was the prisoner — and not this
85 man, who is his twin brother?'

Of course she couldn't. She looked from one to the other and didn't say a
word.

There the big brute sat in the dock with his legs crossed, and there he stood
too at the back of the court and they both stared at Mrs Salmon. She shook
90 her head.

What we saw then was the end of the case. There wasn't a witness
prepared to swear that it was the prisoner he'd seen. And the brother? He had
his alibi too, he was with his wife.

And so the man was acquitted for lack of evidence. But whether — if he did
95 the murder and not his brother — he was punished or not, I don't know. That
extraordinary day had an extraordinary end. I followed Mrs Salmon out of
court and we got wedged in the crowd who were waiting, of course, for the
twins. The police tried to drive the crowd away, but all they could do was keep
the roadway clear for traffic. I learned later that they tried to get the twins to
100 leave by a back way, but they wouldn't. One of them — no one knew which —
said, 'I've been acquitted, haven't I?' and they walked bang out of the front
entrance. Then it happened. I don't know how; though I was only six feet
away. The crowd moved and somehow one of the twins got pushed on to the
road right in front of a bus.
105 He gave a squeal like a rabbit and that was all; he was dead, his skull
smashed just as Mrs Parker's had been. Divine vengeance? I wish I knew.
There was the other Adams getting on his feet from beside the body and
looking straight over at Mrs Salmon. He was crying, but whether he was the
murderer or the innocent man, nobody will ever be able to tell. But if you were
110 Mrs Salmon, could you sleep at night?

Graham Greene, 'The Case for the Defence', *Collected Stories*

The questions which follow are 'objective test' or 'multiple-choice questions' which some GCSE boards will use:

1 For which ONE of the following reasons was the Peckham murder trial probably the strangest that the author ever attended?
A Death struck dramatically to confuse the issue
B The criminal was finally acquitted
C Circumstantial evidence was produced
D The prosecution could not prove its case
E Mistaken identity was the main plea of the defence

2 'Circumstantial evidence', (line 4) given in court is evidence which
A can never be proved as being true
B may be inferred from known facts hard to explain
C can never be introduced into a trial
D is intended to deceive a jury
E can be adapted to suit the case

3 The anxiety of the jurymen described in lines 4 – 6 occurred most probably because they were afraid they might be
A condemning an innocent man
B stopped from hearing all the facts
C releasing a known murderer
D unable to make up their minds
E incapable of understanding the evidence

4 'Crown counsel' (line 7) is the barrister who speaks for the
A court
B witnesses
C jury
D prosecution
E defence

5 The chances of the accused man's being acquitted were thought to be very slight because
A the Crown counsel was very clever
B he did not seem to have an alibi
C the police found him near the murder
D he looked such an evil and violent man
E the witnesses had seen him quite clearly

6 Which of the following was not expected to appear as a witness in the case?
A Mrs Salmon
B Adams's wife
C Henry MacDougall
D Mrs Parker
E Mr Wheeler

7 Which of the following words is nearest in meaning to 'suffused' as it is used in line 22?

A Fixed
B Welling
C Protruding
D Bloodshot
E Shut

8 The author thought that all the witnesses probably 'went in fear' (line 24) after the verdict because they were afraid of

A vengeance from the accused
B being punished by divine justice
C prosecution for perjuring themselves
D disbelieving their own senses in future
E conscience plaguing them for ever

9 It is suggested that Adams 'might as well have committed the crime in broad daylight' (lines 32–3) because he

A had been seen by so many people
B would have been able to see better
C had a good chance of being proved innocent
D would have been able to murder the witnesses
E had succeeded in leaving the murder-scene

10 The Crown's case seemed to rest on proving that

    1 the witnesses had seen him
    2 he had been caught in the act
    3 his face was unmistakable
    4 he had obviously used a hammer
    5 Mrs Salmon was a reliable witness

A 1, 2 and 3 only
B 1, 2 and 4 only
C 1, 3 and 5 only
D 2, 3 and 4 only
E 3, 4 and 5 only

11 Adam's eyes are described as 'pekingese' (line 51) because their main characteristic was that they were

A red
B bulging
C cold
D tearful
E enormous

12 The writer expected the defence counsel to take a line which would

A suggest that Mrs Salmon's observation was not completely reliable
B persuade the jury to feel sorry for the murderer
C show that the crime was not in Adams's nature
D emphasise the gravity of the crime committed
E prove that the case was one of suicide

13 All of the following answers of Mrs Salmon did not help the defence counsel

EXCEPT

  A 'I do remember it, sir.' (line 62)
  B 'I have never had to wear spectacles, sir.' (line 64)
  C 'Fifty-six, sir.' (line 66)
  D 'No, sir. There was moonlight.' (line 71)
  E 'None whatever, sir. It isn't a face one forgets.' (line 76)

14 Counsel most probably made the remark 'No, not the prisoner' (lines 78–9)
because
  A Adams had stood up to be recognised
  B Mrs Salmon was still looking at Adams
  C Adams thought he was being addressed
  D Mrs Salmon seemed to see Adams's face everywhere
  E Adams was obviously the real criminal

15 The most likely reason why Mrs Salmon 'didn't say a word' (lines 86–7)
after seeing Adam's twin that she was
  A ashamed
  B excited
  C angry
  D confused
  E suspicious

16 Lines 88–9 suggest that
  A the twins were constantly changing position
  B Adams's spirit seemed to move from body to body
  C the defence had arranged some kind of trick
  D some occult happening was actually taking place
  E Mrs Salmon though she was seeing double

17 Which of the following is nearest in meaning to 'alibi' as it is used in line 93?
  A Freedom from guilt
  B Excuse for the crime
  C Evidence of being elsewhere
  D Moment of suspicion
  E Change to give testimony

18 Adams was finally acquitted of the charge against him because
  A he had been far too clever for the prosecution
  B no evidence at all had been produced
  C his brother's alibi confused the jury
  D none of the evidence conclusively proved his guilt
  E he had managed convincingly to prove he was innocent

19 'Punished' (line 95) suggests that Adams might have been
 A divinely repaid
 B conscience-stricken
 C subsequently hanged
 D driven insane
 E deliberately murdered

20 All of the following are incontestable facts in the case EXCEPT that the
 A murderer left the scene of the crime after 2.00 a.m.
 B victim was an old lady living next door to Mr Wheeler
 C murder had been committed by one of the Adams twins
 D crime took place just outside the Peckham district
 E person who had been murdered had been battered to death

(*f*) Courts and their proceedings are often included in plays as part of a dramatic
climate. Drama needs a strong element of conflict to be powerful and, of
course, a court scene is therefore essentially dramatic. John Galsworthy
(1867–1933) wrote two important plays on the theme of justice and the law:
The Silver Box and *Justice*.
In the first Galsworthy showed how the massive weight of the law could
allow a rich young man accused of a very serious crime to avoid even being
prosecuted. The second play, *Justice*, dealt with the morality of letting the
law grind down a minor criminal; some see the play as having influenced the
Home Office at the time to relax its uncompromising support of solitary
confinement. Above all, Galsworthy drew the attention of people to the fact
that what is *legally* just may may not be *morally* just. (Do laws have to be
moral or does morality merely confuse the issues involved? Can you think of
any instances where this might have happened in recent times?)
Write a court scene, full of conflicting evidence and personalities, bringing
out the full dramatic impact of the occasion. (Base the play, if you wish, on a
real or imagined trial)

(*g*) Punishment for a crime is seen as having four major purposes:
 – to inflict suffering of some kind on the criminal, as a kind of retribution;
 – to deter others;
 – to protect society from the criminal's activities;
 – to reform the criminal.
What are your thoughts about these and other purposes of punishment?
(You may like to set down your ideas or discuss with others in your English
group such matters as: corporal punishment in schools; capital punishment;
fines; loss of privileges; detention; open and closed prisons, etc. How far
should the punishment fit the crime? Are there some forms of criminal
punishment that a just society could never inflict without changing its very
self? How would you deal with the criminal who offends again and again?)

Here are two poems about the struggle for a better society. The first shows the despair felt by a soldier in 1940 who wondered if war was ever a way to bring it about:

TO A CONSCRIPT OF 1940

A soldier passed me in the freshly-fallen snow,
His footsteps muffled, his face unearthly grey;
And my heart gave a sudden leap
As I gazed on a ghost of five-and-twenty years ago.

I shouted Halt! and my voice had the old accustomed ring
And he obeyed it as it was obeyed
In the shrouded days when I too was one
Of an army of young men marching

Into the unknown. He turned towards me and I said:
'I am one of those who went before you
Five-and-twenty years ago: one of the many who never returned,
Of the many who returned and yet were dead.

We went where you are going, into the rain and mud;
We fought as you will fight
With death and darkness and despair;
We gave what you will give — our brains and our blood.

We think we gave in vain. The world was not renewed.
There was hope in the homestead and anger in the streets
But the old world was restored and we returned
To the dreary field and workshop, and the immemorial feud

Of rich and poor. Our victory was our defeat.
Power was retained where power had been misused
And youth was left to sweep away
The ashes that the fires had strewn beneath our feet.

But one thing we learned: there is no glory in the deed
Until the soldier wears a badge of tarnished braid;
There are heroes who have heard the rally and have seen
The glitter of a garland round their head.

Theirs is the hollow victory. They are deceived.
But you, my brother and my ghost, if you can go
Knowing that there is no reward, no certain use
In all you sacrifice, then honour is reprieved.

To fight without hope is to fight with grace,
The self reconstructed, the false heart repaired.
Then I turned with a smile, and he answered my salute
As he stood against the fretted hedge, which was white like lace.

Herbert Reid

The second poem has at its heart the failure of one group of people to understand another group who had been promised 'a land fit for heroes' after their struggle through four years of bloody warfare during 1914–18. In the 1920s the miners went on a national strike for better wages and conditions but they found themselves struggling through misunderstanding and an unreadiness to see their needs and hopes. A new society is not easy to produce from an old one. Sassoon's poem has an uncomfortable modern message for today:

THE CASE FOR THE MINERS

Something goes wrong with my synthetic brain
When I defend the Strikers and explain
My reasons for not blackguarding the Miners.
'What do you know?' exclaim my fellow-diners
(Peeling their plovers' eggs or lifting glasses
Of mellowed *Chateau Rentier* from the table),
'What do you know about the working classes?'
I strive to hold my own; but I'm unable
To state the case succinctly. Indistinctly
I mumble about World-Emancipation,
Standards of Living, Nationalisation
Of industry; until they get me tangled
In superficial details; goad me on
To unconvincing vagueness. When we've wrangled
From soup to savoury, my temper's gone.

'Why should a miner earn six pounds a week?
Leisure! They'd only spend it in a bar!
Standard of life! You'll never teach them Greek,
Or make them more contented than they are'
That's how my port-flushed friends discuss the Strike.
And that's the reason why I'd almost like
To see them hawking matches in the gutter.

Siegfried Sassoon

(N.B. Siegfried Sassoon, 1886–1967, was a member of the upper classes himself who wrote realistically of life in the trenches in the first world war in both his verse and prose.)

Both these poems deal with frustration and express the disappointment of not being able to create the 'Brave New World' that many people long for. They deal, too, with misunderstanding, selfishness, and the failure of all members of society to work together for the new society.

Write sensitively about your own frustrations as a young person living at the end of a century that has seen many changes, has undergone too many bloodbaths and revolutions, but which still has poverty, prejudice, unemployment, and bleakness in life. If you wish, you may write in verse form, if you feel that a poetic shape to your work will allow you to express your thoughts and feelings more clearly and vividly.

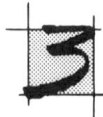

The picture below was published in the colour supplement of a major Sunday newspaper. It shows the plight of refugees in Sudan, driven from their homes by famine and warfare. Use the details it portrays as the basis for *either* a group discussion *or* a report from an individual news reporter on radio on the subject of 'Caring for one's neighbour'.

Some of the topics you may wish to raise may be:
- the suffering of the innocent;
- the injustice of famine and disease;
- the imbalance of resources in the western and third worlds;
- the population growth in undeveloped countries;
- the contrast between politicians and the poor;
- the selfishness of men and women who ignore the desperation of others;
- the need for greater and more imaginative forms of aid;
- the effects of civil war on the population;
- the organisation of care in refugee camps;
- the ways to eliminate social injustices;
- the ideal of world government.

Unit 2

Falling in and out of love

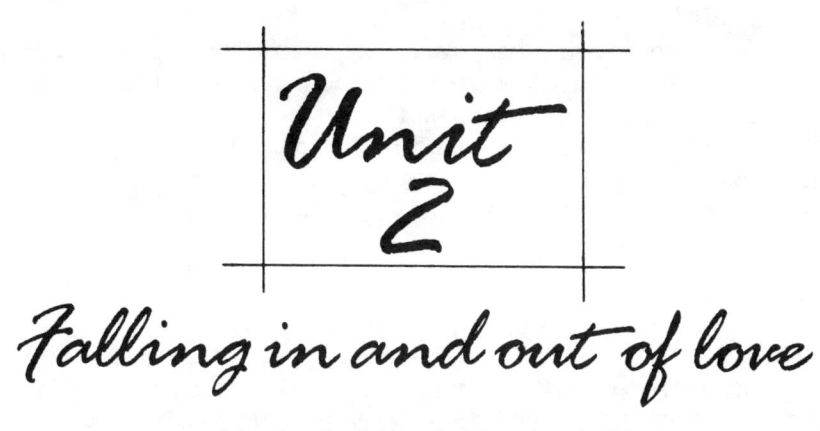

No, there's nothing half so sweet in life
As love's young dream.
Thomas Moore (1779–1852)

Teenage is a time for falling in and out of love. It is also a time for feeling emotions strongly in terms of high elation or deep anguish. Self-discovery and the discovery of others — particularly others of the opposite sex — can be devastating; it is almost always bewildering. This unit is concerned with the fundamental experience of being in love and being in love with love. It demands above all the expression of personal feelings and the growing readiness as well to step back from the situation to see things in new perspectives. The opportunities it presents will demand all the power you have to express yourself from a clear point of view, about a subject with which you can identify, for an audience (quite often yourself) which is clear. In other words, it will demand all your skill in using directed writing.

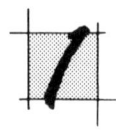

Here are two extracts from the diaries of teenagers about being in love. The first is authentic in the sense that it was written by a fourteen-year-old girl as part of a personal record of her feelings; the second was written by Sue Townsend, but it captures successfully, if somewhat ironically, the inner 'screwed-up-tight' feelings of a teenage boy.

Read them both carefully and then tackle the questions that follow.

Monday, 17th April, 1944

(*a*)   Dear Kitty,

Do you think Daddy and Mummy would approve of my sitting and kissing a boy on a divan — a boy of seventeen and a half and a girl of just under fifteen? I don't really think they would, but I must rely on myself over this. It is so quiet and peaceful to lie in his arms and to dream, it is so thrilling to feel his cheek against mine, it is so lovely to know that there is someone waiting for me. But there is indeed a big 'But' because will Peter be content to leave it at this? I haven't forgotten his promise already, but... he *is* a boy!

I know myself that I'm starting very soon, not even fifteen, and so independent already! It's certainly hard for other people to understand. I know almost for certain that Margot would never kiss a boy unless there had been some talk of an engagement or marriage, but neither Peter nor I have anything like that in mind. I'm sure too that Mummy never touched a man before Daddy. What would my girl friends say about it if they knew that I lay in Peter's arms, my heart against his chest, my head on his shoulder and with his head against mine!

Oh, Anne, how scandalous! But honestly, I don't think it is; we are shut up here, shut away from the world, in fear and anxiety, especially just lately.* Why, then, should we who love each other remain apart? Why should we wait until we have reached a suitable age? Why should we bother?

I have taken it upon myself to look after myself; he would never want to cause me sorrow or pain. Why shouldn't I follow the way my heart leads me, if it makes us both happy? All the same, Kitty, I believe you can sense that I am in doubt. I think it must be my honesty which rebels against doing anything on the sly! Do you think it's my duty to tell Daddy what I'm doing? Do you think we should share our secret with a third person? A lot of beauty would be lost, but would my conscience feel happier? I will discuss it with 'him'.

Oh, yes, there's still so much I want to talk to him about, for I don't see the use of only just cuddling each other. To exchange our thoughts, that shows confidence, and faith in each other; we would both be sure to profit by it!

Yours, Anne.

Anne Frank, *The Diary of Anne Frank*

Saturday, August 8

(*b*)   At 7 a.m. Pandora rang from St Pancras station. She said that due to electrification of the track at Flitwick she would be delayed.

I got dressed and went down to the station, got a platform ticket, waited on platform two for six cold, lonely hours. Went home to find a note from

---

*   Anne and her family were Jews living in a secret annexe in a house in Amsterdam to escape from the Nazis during 1942–44. Finally they were discovered and were sent to concentration camps. Anne died in Bergen-Belsen a few days after her sister in early March 1945.

Pandora. This is what it said:

Adrian,
I confess to feeling heartbroken at your apparent coldness concerning my arrival. I felt sure that we would have an emotional reunion on platform three. But it was not to be.
Adieu,
Pandora.

Went to Pandora's house. Explained. Had an emotional reunion behind her father's tool shed.

Thursday, October 1st

7.30 a.m.
Just woke up to find chin covered in spots! How can I face Pandora?
10 p.m.
Avoided Pandora all day but she caught up with me in school dinners. I tried to eat with my hand over my chin but it proved difficult. I confessed to her during yoghurt. She accepted my disability very calmly. She said it made no difference to our love but I couldn't help thinking that her kisses lacked their usual passion as we were saying goodnight after youth club.

Saturday, October 3rd

Pandora is cooling off. She didn't turn up to Bert's today. I had to do his cleaning on my own.

Went to Sainsbury's as usual in the afternoon; they are selling Christmas cakes. I feel that my life is slipping away.

I am reading *Wuthering Heights*. It is brilliant. If I could get Pandora up somewhere high, I'm sure we could regain our old passion.

Friday, November 13th

Pandora and I had a frank talk about our relationship tonight. She doesn't want to marry me in two years' time!

She wants to have a career instead!

Naturally I am devastated by this blow. I told her I wouldn't mind her having a little job in a cake shop or something after our wedding, but she said she intended to go to university and that the only time she would enter a cake shop would be to buy a large crusty.

Harsh words were exchanged between us. (Hers were harsher than mine.)

Later   *Monday, March 29th*
I ate my school dinner sitting next to Barbara Boyer. She is a truly wonderful girl. She pointed out that Pandora had got a lot of faults. I was forced to agree with her.

Sue Townsend, *The Secret Diary of Adrian Mole aged 13¾*

1 What do the two passages have in common? In what ways do they differ?
2 Which of the two extracts seems more authentic to you? Justify your opinion by referring to details.
3 What differences in style do you notice between the two passages? Give examples to illustrate what you are saying.

4 Imagine that you are (*a*) Peter and (*b*) Pandora writing entries in their own diaries to describe the very incidents mentioned by Anne and Adrian respectively. Bearing in mind that the change of diary writer will alter perspectives, write up your own diary entries.

5 Write some entries for your own personal diary setting out events during the period when you were falling in and/or out of love. (Don't try to imitate the language or the style of the extracts written by Anne Frank and Adrian Mole.)

The next two extracts are written by well-known poets re-telling incidents in their teenage lives. Both passages deal with the uncertainties, excitement, and frustrations of meeting the opposite sex. Read them carefully and then consider the questions which follow them.

The first is by Dannie Abse (born 1923) and is taken from his autobiography, *Ash on a Young Man's Sleeve*:

(*a*) Through the November streets we roamed: Bob, Basil, Ken, Alun (who had just moved into the district) and myself, the youngest. We hung round Lydia Pike's house just to receive a glimpse of her. Alun hadn't seen her yet. We waited expectantly.

'She goes to The Parade,' volunteered Bob.

'The Parade's the girls' high school,' I informed Alun.

'I'm not interested in women,' said Alun.

'Nor am I,' said Bob with alacrity.

'Nor am I,' said Basil.

'Nor am I,' said Ken.

They looked at me anxiously.

'Nor am I,' I said.

We stood there at the corner, half-way up Cyncoed Hill, the other side of the disused quarry. The new row of grey shaled houses overlooked the chimney pots of Cardiff as they slanted down to the Bristol Channel. Soon they would erase the view by building houses on the south side of the street, and so destroy the feeling one had of almost being in the country; for further down the road, to the east, the tarmac came abruptly to an end and a stony skeleton of a path continued onwards through a gate, into a field, following a lovers' walk past a famous spot where a middle-aged woman, a few years before, had been casually murdered.

Lydia Pike's house, with its garage and front lawn, stood unfriendly behind us. And its blind windows gazed out, over the smoky beer-coloured weather of autumn, at the distant sea on which some child artist had drawn the silhouette of a static cardboard ship.

'Let's go then,' said Alun.

'No point in waiting here,' said Basil.

'Absolutely no point,' I said.

'Stupid, isn't it?' said Ken.

'Besides,' said Bob, 'what would we do if she came?'

'Ask her for a date,' said Basil.

'Bet you wouldn't,' screamed Bob.

'Bet you a shilling,' I said.

'I'm not interested in women,' said Alun.

'If I was interested I'd make a date,' Basil pronounced.
'Bet you wouldn't,' I said.
'Let's go,' said Alun. 'None of us are interested.'
'Where'll we go?' Ken asked.
'Nowhere to go,' Bob said sadly.
'May as well stay here,' I said.
'You're a bunch of ladies' men,' jeered Alun. 'Women,' he added knowingly. Women — *Ach y fu*.'
'Well, where'll we go?' asked Basil.
'Anywhere, but let's go. It's cold standing about,' said Alun.

Lydia Pike came round the corner on her own. We politely moved out of the way, clearing the pavement. She minced past us in her black sweater, nose tilted in the air, her blown golden hair falling like water over the back of her shoulders. She ran up the steps, gave us a dazzling look, and in a moment she had disappeared inside the house, and not one of us had spoken a word.
'Let's go,' said Basil.
'Yes,' said Bob.
'Silly waiting here,' I said.

Daniel Abse, Ash on a Young Man's Sleeve

The second passage is also from an autobiography, *Cider with Rosie* by Laurie Lee in 1959:

(b) A year or so later occurred the Brith Wood rape. If it could be said to have occurred. We planned the rape a week before, up in the builder's stable. The stable's thick air of mouldy chaff, dry leather and rotting straw, its acid floors and unwashed darkness provided the atmosphere we needed. We met there regularly to play cards and scratch and whistle and talk about girls.

There were about half a dozen of us that morning, including Walt Kerry, Bill Shepherd, Sixpence the Tanner, Boney and Clergy Green. The valley outside, seen through the open door, was crawling with April rain. We sat round on buckets sucking strips of harness. Then suddenly Bill Shepherd came out with it.

'Here,' he said. 'Listen. I got'n idea.'

He dropped his voice into a furry whisper and drew us into a circle.

'You know that Lizzy Berkeley, don't you?' he said. 'She'd do,'he said. 'She's daft in the 'ead. She'd be all right, y'know.'

We thought about Lizzy and it was true enough; she was daft about religion. A short, plump girl of about sixteen, with large blue-bottle-eyes, she used to walk in Brith Wood with a handful of crayons writing texts on the trunks of beech trees. Huge rainbow letters on the smooth green bark, saying 'JESUS LOVES ME, NOW.'

'I seen 'er Sunday,' said Walt, 'an' she was at it then.'
'She's always at it,' said Boney.
'Jerusalem!' said Clergy in his pulpit voice.
'Well, 'ow about it?' said Bill. 'It's like this, see. Blummin'-well simple.' We listened and held our breath. 'After church Sunday mornin' we nips up to the wood. An' when'er comes back from chapel — we got 'er.'

We all breathed out. We saw it clearly. We saw her coming alone through the Sunday wood, chalk-coloured Lizzy, unsuspecting and holy, in the bundle of her clothes and body. We saw her come walking through her text-chalked trees, blindly, straight into our hands.

'She'd 'oller,' said Boney.

'She's too batty,' said Bill.

'She'd think I was one of the 'possles.'

Clergy gave his whinnying, nervous giggle, and Boney rolled on the floor.

'You all on, then?' Bill whispered. 'Wha's say? 'Ow about it? It'll half be a stunt, you watch.'

We none of us answered, but we all felt committed.

On Sunday morning we trooped from the church and signalled to each other with our eyebrows. The morning was damp with a springtime sun. We nodded, winked, and jerked our heads, then made our separate ways to the wood. When we gathered at last at the point of ambush, the bounce had somehow gone out of us. We were tense and silent; nobody spoke. We lay low as arranged and waited.

We waited a long time. Birds sang, squirrels chattered, the sun shone; but nobody came. We began to cheer up and giggle.

'She ain't comin', said someone. 'She seen Bill first.'

'She seen 'im and gone screamin' 'ome.'

''Er's lucky, then. I'd 'ave made 'er 'oller.'

'I'd 'ave run 'er up a tree.'

We were savage and happy, as though we'd won a battle. But we waited a little longer.

'Sod it,' said Bill. 'Let's push off. Come on.' And we were all of us glad he'd said it.

At that moment we saw her, walking dumpily up the path, solemn in her little straw hat. Bill and Boney went sickly pale and watched her in utter misery. She approached us slowly, a small fat doll, shafts of sunlight stroking her dress. None of us moved as she drew level with us; we just looked at Bill and Boney. They returned our looks with a kind of abject despair and slowly got to their feet.

What happened was clumsy, quick and meaningless; silent, like a very old film. The two boys went loping down the bank and barred the plump girl's way. She came to a halt and they all stared at each other... The key moment of our fantasy; and trivial. After a gawky pause, Bill shuffled towards her and laid a hand on her shoulder. She hit him twice with her bag of crayons, stiffly, with the jerk of a puppet. Then she turned, fell down, got up, looked round, and trotted away through the trees.

Bill and Boney did nothing to stop her; they slumped and just watched her go. And the last we saw of our virgin Lizzy was a small round figure, like a rubber ball, bouncing downhill out of sight.

After that, we just melted away through the wood separately, in opposite directions. I dawdled home slowly, whistling aimless tunes and throwing stones at stumps and gateposts. What had happened that morning was impossible to say. But we never spoke of it again.

Laurie Lee, *Cider with Rosie*

1 Both these passages are seen from boys' points of view. Re-write the incidents as they might have been seen through the eyes of Lydia Pike and Lizzy Berkeley respectively.

2 (*a*) Both passages contain descriptions of the surroundings. How do these descriptions help the narrative? Can you see any similarities in the kinds of descriptions both poets use?

   (*b*) Pick out from the passages some vivid comparisons used by the poets (e.g. 'the smoky beer-coloured weather of autumn'). Say what you think each means and try to suggest reasons why the writers have used them.

3 Both passages have a similar shape. Can you say what this shape is? Then try to write an account of an encounter you and your friends have had with a member of the opposite sex using a similar structure to that of the passages for your narrative.

4 Both writers try to re-live the incidents seen through their eyes as teenagers. Try to re-write one of the passages as it might have appeared had the writer used a different approach and written from his point of view as a middle-aged man.

5 Give an account of any other narrative *or* short story *or* autobiography you have read which deals with harmless teenage fantasies about the opposite sex.

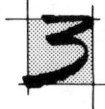

The problems of the relationship between a boy and a girl are frequently featured in the pages of some magazines, newspapers, and journals, e.g.

> *I went out for a date for the first time last week. I'm 15. When the boy kissed me I felt sick, and whenever I think about it I feel the same. Do you think there is something wrong with me?*
> Perhaps you'd dreamed of your first kiss as something out of this world and now you've discovered that, like everything else which involves two people, a kiss depends on how you feel about the other person and where, when and how it happens. If this one was rather insensitively planted on you by a boy you don't know very well then it could quite easily be no pleasure at all. But don't let this put you off kissing or the boy — just have a bit more say about when you're kissed so that it happens when *you* want it too.

Write three different letters, each setting out a problem of relationships encountered with the opposite sex during adolescence. Draft, too, sensible replies which are based on your own experience of coping with such difficulties.

The story of *Romeo and Juliet* is, perhaps, the best known story of the tragic love of young people. Shakespeare's play deals with the starcross'd Romeo, son of Lord Montague, and Juliet, daughter of Lord Capulet. The enmity of the two families leads to the early deaths of the young people. In the late nineteenth century a Swiss novelist, Gottfried Keller, wrote *A Village Romeo and Juliet* (translated by P.B. Thomas, 1955) using the theme of the quarrel between two successful peasants, Manz and Marti, whose children, Sali and Vrenchen, cannot find happiness together because of the family feud. After a single gloriously happy day spent together they commit suicide. The newspapers report the event only in terms of the way morals have degenerated but the love of Sali and Vrenchen was too strong for them either to marry or to be separated.

Think carefully about the Romeo and Juliet kind of story and then write one of your own in which two young people find themselves in a hopeless situation about their relationship because of family feuding, social conditions, or some other kind of impediment and come to an untimely tragic end.
(NB. You might also like to read R. D. Blackmore's story *Lorna Doone* in which John Ridd, at the age of 12, has his father murdered by the Doone family but falls later in love with Lorna, a girl kidnapped by, and living with, the Doones and engaged to Carver Doone. Lorna returns John's love and then dramatically she is found to be heiress to a fortune; at the altar, just as John and Lorna are married, Carver Doone shoots her and …)

 It is in poetry that the most poignant expression of love unreturned and the most ecstatic expression of love fulfilled is to be found. Often surprise and humour creep into love poetry, too. Read and consider these two poems:

(*a*) LOVE

The difficult part of love
Is being selfish enough,
Is having the blind persistence
To upset someone's existence
Just for your own sake -
What cheek it must take.

And then the unselfish side
Who can be satisfied
Putting someone else first,
So that you come off worst?
My life is for me:
As well deny gravity.

Yet vicious or virtuous
Love still suits most of us;
Only the bleeder who
Can't manage either view
Is ever wholly rebuffed -
And he can get stuffed.

Philip Larkin

(*b*) A SLICE OF WEDDING CAKE

Why have such scores of lovely, gifted girls
    Married impossible men
Simple self-sacrifice may be ruled out,
    And missionary endeavour, nine times out of ten.

Repeat 'impossible men'; not merely rustic
   Foul-tempered or depraved
(Dramatic foils chosen to show the world
   How well women behave, and always have behaved).

Impossible men: idle, illiterate,
   Self-pitying, dirty, sly,
For whose appearance even in City parks
   Excuses must be made to casual passers-by.

Has God's supply of tolerable husbands
   Fallen, in fact, so low?
Or do I always over-value women
   At the expense of man?
               Do I?

               It might be so.

                  Robert Graves

Compile your own short anthology of poems on love and try to group them around themes such as 'tragic love', 'constancy', 'love and hope', 'disappointment', etc.

   Add to the anthology some poems on the subject of *Love* you might have written yourself.

 Whilst the subject of love is treated seriously by writers, it has also been the subject of much fun:

THE SORROWS OF WERTHER

Werther had a love for Charlotte
   Such as words could never utter;
Would you know how first he met her?
   She was cutting bread and butter.

Charlotte was a married lady,
   And a moral man was Werther,
And for all the wealth of Indies,
   Would do nothing to hurt her.

So he sigh'd and pined and ogled,
   And his passion boil'd and bubbled,
Till he blew his silly brains out,
   And no more was by it troubled.

Charlotte, having seen his body
   Borne before her on a shutter,
Like a well-conducted person,
   Went on cutting bread and butter.

            W. M. Thackeray

Can you devise a tune for the story of Werther — or perhaps you can sing it to a guitar accompaniment? The following story has also been set to music. See if you can find the tune (or invent one) for the verses sung in Victorian music-halls:

POLLY PERKINS

I am a broken-hearted milkman, in grief I'm arrayed,
Through keeping of the company of a young servant maid,
Who lived on board and wages the house to keep clean
In a gentleman's family near Paddington Green.

Chorus:
    She was as beautiful as a butterfly
        And as proud as a Queen
    Was pretty little Polly Perkins of
        Paddington Green.

She'd an ankle like an antelope and step like a deer,
A voice like a blackbird, so mellow and clear,
Her hair hung in ringlets so beautiful and long,
I thought that she loved me but found I was wrong.

When I'd rattle in the morning and cry 'milk below',
At the sound of my milk-cans her face she would show
With a smile upon her countenance and laugh in her eye;
If I thought she'd have loved me, I'd have laid down to die.

When I asked her to marry me she said 'Oh! what stuff',
And told me to 'drop it', for she had quite enough
Of my nonsense' — at the same time I'd been very kind,
But to marry a milkman she didn't feel inclined.

'Oh the man that has me must have silver and gold,
A chariot to ride in and be handsome and bold,
His hair must be curly as any watch spring,
And his whiskers as big as a brush for clothing.'

The words that she uttered went straight through my heart,
I sobbed and I sighed, and straight did depart;
With a tear on my eyelid as big as a bean,
Bidding good-bye to Polly and Paddington Green.

In six months she married, — this hard-hearted girl, —
But it was not a Wi-count, and it was not a Nearl,
It was not a 'Baronite', but a shade or two wuss,
It was a bow-legged conductor of a twopenny bus.

Anon.

Write a short farcical scene in dramatic form embodying this material from the song. If you prefer it, sketch out a mimed sequence that could accompany the song.

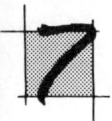

The photograph below is a still from a famous film, Roger Leenhardt's *Les Dernières Vacances* ('The Last Holidays') about the growing awareness of each other of two young people who have grown up together but never felt physically attracted to each other particularly before. Try to write a film script for a scene centred on the photograph. (Keep the dialogue simple and sincere.)

Unit 3

Time warps

Time present and time past
Are both perhaps present in time future,
And time future contained in time past.
T. S. Eliot, *Four Quartets: Burnt Norton*

The idea of moving back or forwards in time from the present has always held a fascination for men and women. Some thinkers have suggested that only the past and the future really exist; the present merely marks the dividing line where the future becomes the past.

However, history and science fiction have both concerned themselves with the study of crossing the boundaries of time that we call 'now' or 'the present'. Perhaps the best-known work using the theme of travelling in time is H. G. Wells's *The Time Machine* (1895) which is an allegory on the late nineteenth century two races of men, the rich and the poor; Wells sets his story in the year 802701 and shows a society divided into two: the Morlocks who live and work underground and the Eloi, a decadent social group. More recently Arthur C. Clarke's *2001: A Space Odyssey* (1968) has used the theme of travelling forward in time within a science-fiction context.

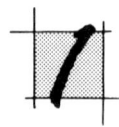

Consider the following passage by H. G. Wells and the extracts from Philip José Farmer's science-fiction writing carefully. Notice particularly how they lead the reader's imagination to accept the notion of time travel by taking familiar details and using them in new contexts:

(*a*) It was ten o'clock today that the first of all Time Machines began its career. I gave it a last tap, tried all the screws again, put one more drop of oil on the quartz rod, and sat myself in the saddle. I suppose a suicide who holds a pistol to his skull feels much the same wonder at what will come next as I felt then. I took the starting lever in one hand and the stopping one in the other, pressed the first, and almost immediately the second. I seemed to reel; I felt a nightmare sensation of falling; and, looking round, I saw the laboratory exactly as before. Had anything happened? For a moment I suspected that my intellect had tricked me. Then I noted the clock. A moment before, as it seemed, it had stood at a minute or so past ten; now it was nearly half-past three.

I drew a breath, set my teeth, gripped the starting lever with both hands, and went off with a thud. The laboratory got hazy and went dark. Mrs Watchets came in and walked, apparently without seeing me, towards the garden door. I suppose it took her a minute or so to traverse the place, but to me she seemed to shoot across the room like a rocket. I pressed the lever over to its extreme position. The night came like the turning-out of a lamp, and in another moment came tomorrow. The laboratory grew faint and hazy, then fainter and fainter. Tomorrow night came back, then day again, night again, day again, faster and faster still. An eddying murmur filled my ears, and a strange dumb confusedness descended on my mind.

I am afraid I cannot convey the peculiar sensations of time travelling. They are excessively unpleasant. There is a feeling exactly like that one has upon a switchback — of a helpless headlong motion! I felt the same horrible anticipation, too, of an imminent smash. As I put on pace, night followed day like the flapping of a black wing. The dim suggestion of the laboratory seemed presently to fall away from me, and I saw the sun hopping swiftly across the sky, leaping it every minute, and every minute marking a day.

I suppose the laboratory had been destroyed and I had come into the open air. I had a dim impression of scaffolding, but I was already going too fast to be conscious of any moving things. The slowest snail that ever crawled dashed by too fast for me...

The landscape was misty and vague. I was still on the hillside upon which this house now stands, and the shoulder rose above me grey and dim. I saw trees growing and changing like puffs of vapour, now brown, now green; they grew, spread, shivered, and passed away. I saw huge buildings rise up faint and fair and pass like dreams. The whole surface of the earth seemed changed — melting and flowing under my eyes. The little hands upon the dials that registered my speed raced round faster and faster. Presently I noted that the sun belt swayed up and down, from solstice to solstice, in a minute or less, and that consequently my pace was over a year a minute...

H.G. Wells, *The Time Machine*

(The changes brought about by swift time changes remind a modern reader of picture sequences of flowers in bud opening and dying with the help of timed photography or of the pictures seen on a television set when the video-recorder is run fast forwards or backwards.)

(*b*) Philip José Farmer is a science-fiction writer who has used many ingenious ways of handling 'time-warps' or movements backwards and forwards in fiction. One story, (*The Stone God Awakens*, 1970) uses the device of the 'matter-freezer': 'The device was capable of stopping for an indeterminate time all atomic movements in a piece of matter. The molecules and the atoms, and the parts that made up the atoms — the protons, neutrons, and so forth — would cease all motion'. A bacterium subjected to the energy complex rayed out by the matter-freezer would become a microscopic statue. It would be as if made of stone but of an indestructible stone. Nothing — acids, explosives, atomic radiation, great heat — could destroy it... Also, there was not even a theory as to how the 'petrified' matter could be 'depetrified'. And so aeons passed and then the stone becomes depetrified and the time warp has occurred. Another of his stories begins: 'The first time that Sir Thomas Malory died was on Earth in A.D. 1471. The English knight got through the terrible weeks after Resurrection Day without too many body wounds, though he suffered grievously from spiritual shock' — and so a character from history finds himself in a new period (*The Magic Labyrinth*, 1980). The opening of *Strange Relations*, 1960, is dramatic:

'Look mother. The clock is running backwards.' Eddie Fetts pointed to the hands on the pilot room dial. Dr Paula Fetts said, the crash must have reversed it.'
'How could it do that?'
'I can't tell you. I don't know everything, son.'
'Oh!'
'Well, don't look at me so disappointedly. I'm a pathologist, not an electrician.'
'Don't be so cross, mother. I can't stand it. Not now.'

Philip José Farmer, *Strange Relations*

1. Devise an opening paragraph for a short story which deals with a period in the past or in the future and contains a device which allows someone from the present to move backwards or forwards in time. Are you able to continue the story without losing your reader's willingness to accept the device you choose as a way of telling it?
2. Take the basic concept of 'a time machine' or one of the ways of producing a time warp used by Philip José Farmer described above to narrate an important event from the past, e.g. a world flood, an historical battle, a revolution, a religious revival, the burning of Rome, *etc.*
3. Devise a way of bringing a person from the past into the present and then let the person tell his or her own story and reactions to life today.

An **autobiography** is a way of allowing a writer to speak of reactions to past incidents in his or her life. Here are three such incidents.

(*a*) The first is by Peter Ustinov telling of the birth of his daughter:

On July 25th, 1945, our daughter Tamara was born at the Woolavington wing of the Middlesex Hospital in London. She is now a creature of grace and charm, with an expression ever youthful and delicate. Then she was entirely bald, a physical feature she retained for an alarming length of time, and her face had about it much of the secrecy and doggedness of a Soviet field-marshal. As I looked at her, trying to kindle feelings of paternity which are entirely intellectual with such tiny children, she stared straight back at me with surprisingly steady blue eyes as though awaiting a complete confession.

My confusion at this inquisatorial gaze was checked by the remark of a swarthy gentleman next to me, who was gazing for the first time at his daughter, in the next slot on the hors-d'oeuvre tray. His girl had a full head of black hair and carried an expression of irritation on her small features, as though she couldn't get her castanets to click. 'They're all much of a muchness, aren't they?' he said, heaving with fraternity.

Peter Ustinov, *Dear Me*

(*b*) The second is a poem in which a father recalls an incident when his son was still very young:

A CHILD HALF-ASLEEP

Stealthily parting the small-hours silence,
A hardly-embodied figment of his brain
Comes down to sit with me
As I work late.
Flat-footed, as though his legs and feet
Were still asleep.

He sits on a stool,
Staring into the fire,
His dummy dangling.

Fire ignites the small coals of his eyes:
It stares back through the holes
Into his head, into the darkness.

I ask what woke him.

'A wolf dreamed me,' he says.

Tony Connor

(*c*) The third passage is from Dylan Thomas's *Quite Early One Morning* (1954) and recalls incidents from his boyhood.

Behind the school was a narrow lane where only the oldest and boldest threw pebbles at windows, scuffled and boasted, fibbed about their relations:
'My father's got a chauffeur.'
'What's he want a chauffeur for, he hasn't got a car?'
'My father's the richest man in the town.'
'My father's the richest man in Wales.'
'My father owns the world.'
And swopped gob-stoppers for slings, old knives for marbles, kite string for foreign stamps.
The lane was always the place to tell your secrets; if you did not have any, you invented them: occasionally now I dream that I am turning out of school into the lane of confidences when I say to the boys of my class, 'At last, I have a real secret.'
'What is it? What is it?'
'I can fly.'
And when they do not believe me, I flap my arms and slowly leave the ground, only a few inches at first, then gaining air until I fly waving my cap level with the upper windows of the school, peering in until the mistress at the piano screams and the metronome falls to the ground and stops, and there is no more time.

Dylan Thomas, *Quite Early One Morning*

1. Which of these three passages do you find the most humorous? By quoting from the one you choose (and perhaps from the others, too) show why you think this is.
2. Choose the passage you like best and then continue it (in a similar style, if you wish) to describe another following incident.
3. Describe a humorous incident from your own childhood as you look back; use some of the methods of description used by the writers of the three passages if they will help you to write vividly.
4. Re-tell one of the events described in the passage from the point of view of one of the other people involved in it.
5. Write an account of your life as it is now as you might well write it looking back on it in fifty years' time.

On page 47 is a picture of Sir Winston Churchill visiting the ruins of Coventry Cathedral bombed during the horrific raid on the town in 1940 by German bombers. 1940 was an important year in the history of Europe and indeed of the world. Here is a chart setting out the major events of that year; it lists not only details of the war but other major happenings too:

History	*Literature and the Arts*	*Science and Other Events*
German invasion of Denmark, Norway, France and Holland. Evacuation from Dunkirk. Battle of Britain. Italy declared war on Britain and France: France invaded. British offensive against Italians in North Africa. Japan joined Rome–Berlin axis. Churchill appointed head of a coalition ministry. Germans occupied Channel Islands. President Roosevelt elected for a third term. Russia re-occupied Latvia, Lithuania, Esthonia. Trotsky assassinated in Mexico.	G.Greene, *The Power and the Glory*. Hemingway, *For Whom the Bell Tolls*. C.S.Lewis, *The Problem of Pain*. Dylan Thomas, *Portrait of the Artist as a Young Dog*. M.Sholokhov, *The Silent Don*. Duke Ellington's orchestral Jazz. Hitchcock's film *Rebecca*. Matisse, Picasso, Moore: major paintings. George VI instituted the George Cross and George Medal. Walt Disney's *Fantasia*.	Home Guard formed. Purchase Tax introduced. Food rationing introduced. Shell Oil Co. designed new combustion chamber for jet engines. Blood plasma used instead of red blood for transfusions. SS Queen Elizabeth launched. Discovery of Lascaux caves in France with their cave drawings. Successful experiments with penicillin.

Summary based on L.C. Pascoe and others, *Encyclopaedia of Dates and Events*, Teach Yourself Books, 1968, pages 622–624.

1. Choose any one of these events and find out all you can about it. Then make it a work project in which you set out and document all that you discover.
2. Visit an old person or talk to a relative who remembers 1940 vividly. Make a report for your history teacher or tutor of what you learn about the war from him or her.
3. Take one of the books, paintings, or pieces of music produced in 1940 and write a full account of it. Mention particularly what reflection of the age in which it was written it contains.

4. Prepare for your history folder a similar chart with the headings '*History*', '*Literature and the Arts*', '*Science and other events*' for any one year during your own lifetime. Then write your own personal memories of that year in the form of an autobiography.
5. On a cassette-recorder, or with the help of the school's language laboratory, record an interview between you and a friend playing the role of a man or woman from a previous or future century. You may play the role either of the interviewer of the person being interviewed. (Research the context and the details used in the interview very carefully before you begin your recording. Avoid sticking closely to a prepared script.)

English Literature is full of examples of historical novels and romances. Amongst the best known are those of Sir Walter Scott, especially *Ivanhoe* (1819) set in the times of the Normans, *Quentin Durward* (1823) set in fifteenth-century France and *The Fortunes of Nigel* (1822) set in the England of James I. Most historical novels contain real historical incidents. Dickens's *A Tale of Two Cities* (1859) deals with events during the French Revolution. Other famous writers who wrote historical novels were Thackeray, Charles Reade, Charles Kingsley, Thomas Hardy, Balzac, Tolstoy, and more recently Georgette Heyer, Naomi Mitchinson, William Golding, and Mary Renault.

About 1970 the term 'faction' was invented to describe the stories being written which were based on fact. The term was new but the idea was not. Daniel Defoe wrote a fictional account of events in London 1644–65, *A Journal of the Plague Year* (1722); it is worth comparing a brief extract from this book with the genuine eye-witness account of the same years in Samuel Pepys' *Diary*: both are concerned with escapes from houses 'shut up' because of the plague they contained:

(*a*) Many such escapes were made out of infected houses, as particularly when the watchman was sent of some errand; for it was his business to go of any errand that the family sent him of; that is to say, necessaries, such as food and physic; to fetch physicians, if they would come, or surgeons, or nurses, or to order the dead-cart and the like; but with this condition, too, that when he went he was to lock up the outer door of the house and take the key away with him. To evade this, and cheat the watchmen, people got two or three keys made to their locks, or they found ways to unscrew the locks such as were screwed on, and so take off the lock, being in the inside of the house, and while they sent away the watchman to the market, to the bakehouse, or for one trifle or another, open the door and go out as often as they pleased. But this being found out, the officers afterwards had orders to padlock up the doors on the outside, and place bolts on them as they thought fit.

Daniel Defoe, *A Journal of the Plague Year*

(*b*)   September 3rd (Lord's Day), 1665

Among other stories was one very passionate, methought, of a
complaint brought against a man in the toune for taking a child from
London from an infected house. Alderman Hooker told us it was the
child of a very able citizen in Gracious Street, a saddler, who had buried
all the rest of his children of the plague, and himself and wife now being
shut up and in despair of escaping, did desire only to save the life of this
little child; and so prevailed to have it received stark-naked into the arms
of a friend, who brought it (having put it into new fresh clothes) to
Greenwich; where upon hearing the story, we did agree it should be
permitted to be received and kept in the toune.

Samuel Pepys, *Diary*

1. Find out all you can about the Plague in London in 1665 and then write an
account of what you discover.
2. Which of these two accounts gives the most graphic account of being shut up
in a house during an outbreak of the Plague? Try to explain why you think
this is so.
3. Write a short scene for a one-act play setting out life as it was in London in
1665. You may like to 'invent' a family undergoing all the strains of living
closely together with a member of the family discovering he or she has caught
the Plague.
4. Discuss with the rest of your English group what it is you consider to be the
biggest threat to your well-being today. (In 1665 the Plague must have been at
the top of the list for those living in London!)
5. Here is a poem about a threat to everyone in the future; its very ordinariness
makes it frightening. Read it carefully and then write down your reactions to
it. (You may wish to write a poem of your own about a future threat to your
own happiness.)

THE RESPONSIBILITY

I am the man who gives the nod,
If it should come, to use the Bomb.

I am the man who spreads the word
From him to them if it should come.

I am the man who gets the word
From him who spreads the word from him.

I am the man who drops the Bomb
If ordered by the one who's heard
From him who merely spreads the word
The first one gives if it should come.

I am the man who loads the Bomb
That he must drop should order come
From him who gets the word passed on
By one who waits to hear from *him*.

I am the man who makes the Bomb
That he must load for him to drop
If told by one who gets the word
From one who passes it from *him*.

I am the man who fills the till,
Who pays the tax, who foots the bill
That guarantees the Bomb he makes
For him to load for him to drop
If orders come from one who gets
The word passed on to him by one
Who waits to hear it from the man
Who gives the word to use the Bomb.

I am the man behind it all;
I am the one responsible.

Peter Appleton

 It is often said of some old people that they 'live in the past' and certainly for some the past does seem more real than the present. Pip's visit to Miss Havisham in *Great Expectations* by Charles Dickens or Dylan Thomas's visit to his grandfather in *The Portrait of the Artist as a Young Dog* are memorable instances in literature that spring quickly to mind. Can you think of others?

Consider the following *two* poems. One is a parody of the other; that is, the second deliberately imitates the first to make the first seem ridiculous.

(*a*) THE OLD MAN'S COMFORTS AND HOW HE GAINED THEM

You are old, Father William, the young man cried,
The few locks which are left you are grey;
You are hale, Father William, a hearty old man,
Now tell me the reason, I pray.

In the days of my youth, Father William replied,
I remember that youth would fly fast,
And abused not my health and my vigour at first,
That I never might need them at last.

You are old, Father William, the young man cried,
And pleasures with youth pass away;
And yet you lament not the days that are gone,
Now tell me the reason, I pray.

In the days of my youth, Father William replied,
I remembered that youth could not last;
I thought of the future, whatever I did,
That I never might grieve for the past.

You are old, Father William, the young man cried,
And life must be hastening away;
You are cheerful, and love to converse upon death,
Now tell me the reason, I pray.

I am cheerful young man, Father William replied,
Let the cause thy attention engage;
In the days of my youth I remembered my God!
And he hath not forgotten my age.

Robert Southey (1799)

(*b*)   FATHER WILLIAM

'Repeat "You are old, Father William" , ' said the Caterpillar. Alice folded her hands, and began:

'You are old, Father William,' the young man said,
And your hair has become very white;
And yet you incessantly stand on your head—
Do you think, at your age, it is right?

'In my youth,' Father William replied to his son,
'I feared it might injure the brain;
But, now that I'm perfectly sure I have none,
Why, I do it again and again.'

'You are old,' said the youth, 'as I mentioned before,
And have grown most uncommonly fat;
Yet you turned a back-somersault in at the door—
Pray, what is the reason for that?'

'In my youth,' said the sage, as he shook his grey locks,
'I kept all my limbs very supple
By the use of this ointment—one shilling the box—
Allow me to sell you a couple?'

'You are old,' said the youth, 'and your jaws are too weak
For anything tougher than suet;
Yet you finished the goose, with the bones and the beak—
Pray, how did you manage to do it?'

'In my youth,' said his father, 'I took to the law,
And argued each case with my wife;
And the muscular strength, which it gave to my jaw
Has lasted the rest of my life.'

'You are old,' said the youth, 'one would hardly suppose
That your eye was as steady as ever;
Yet you balanced an eel on the end of your nose—
What made you so awfully clever?'

'I have answered three questions, and that is enough,'
Said his father, 'Don't give yourself airs!
Do you think I can listen all day to such stuff?
Be off, or I'll kick you down-stairs.'

'That is not said right,' said the Caterpillar.
'Not *quite* right, I'm afraid,' said Alice, timidly; 'some of the words have got altered.'
'It is wrong from beginning to end,' said the Caterpillar decidedly, and there was silence for some minutes.

Lewis Carroll, *Alice's Adventures in Wonderland* (1865)

1. Write a parody of a poem you know well in order to create a similar humorous effect. (Keep the style and the shape of the poem the same as far as you can.)
2. Discuss in your English group some of the problems and pleasures you have found in meeting old people — either members of your own families or old people who need help.
3. Devise a project with some others in your group how to help some lonely, house-ridden old people in your area. Then set out a plan of what you all intend to do.
4. Write a short story in which an old person recalls his or her past. Use 'flashbacks' in your story to shift the reader back from the present into the past. (Emily Brontë's famous novel *Wuthering Heights* uses this technique brilliantly in telling its romantic love story of Heathcliff and Catherine.)
5. Try to visit a local hospital where old people are looked after. Talk to the nurses and the doctors about the problems they have and talk to the old people about the problems they have. (Remember that in asking the old to recall their past it is usually more important to listen than to talk too much.) Write up an account of the experiences you had for your course-work file.

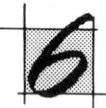 Finally there is a strange but true story of a real time warp. On 25 January 1972, Sergeant Shoichi Yokoi at the age of 56, a member of the Japanese Imperial Army, was captured on the Pacific Island of Guam after 28 years in hiding refusing to surrender to the enemy.

Yokoi was heavily bearded when found, wearing trousers and jacket made from tree and bark fibre. He had been a tailor when conscripted in 1941, and used a pair of scissors he had had throughout the war to shape the clothes and to cut his hair. He told reporters that he had lived since the war on a diet of nuts, breadfruit, mangoes, papaya, shrimps, snails, rats and frogs. He had never heard either of the atomic bomb, or of television, and stared in disbelief when told that a jet aircraft could return him to his home town Nagoya in three hours.

For 28 years Sergeant Yokoi had lived in a time warp. He said that he and two other Japanese fled into the jungles of Guam when American troops recaptured the island in 1944. They knew that on Guam, at least, the war was over, because of leaflets they found scattered through the jungle. Yokoi and his two comrades held out, fearing they might be executed if they surrendered. About eight years before his discovery Yokoi had gone to the cave where the other two had been living, and found them dead. 'I believe they died of starvation,' he said.

Yokoi slept only fitfully after his discovery, crouching against a wall in a position which recalled the way he had slept in his jungle hideout. During the day he brooded, holding his head in his hands. He broke out in cold sweats and muttered that a ghost was standing at his bedside, admonishing him for having deserted his comrades. Doctors were alarmed about his mental condition. A Japanese journalist reported: 'He seems to be making a desperate effort to find an exit from the "time tunnel" that separates his former world from today's civilisation.'

Guam itself had now become a popular resort for Japanese tourists. When Yokoi saw honeymooning couples, the men with long hair, the girls in hot pants, he stared in disbelief: 'Are they really Japanese?' he asked. The reporters themselves were an enigma to him. 'You are different Japanese.' he said. 'There must be other Japanese people.'

This real-life story reminds readers of Washington Irving's story of Rip Van Winkle (published in 1820) in which a man, seeking to escape from his nagging wife, went on a ramble in the Catskill Mountains, fell asleep for twenty years, and woke to find everything changed and his wife dead. The fiction is even older. Gregory of Tours (*c*. 540–94) and the *Koran* (authorized version published in the mid-seventh century) both narrate the story of the Seven Sleepers of Ephesus, seven Christian young men who fled from the persecution of Darius (AD 250) and hid in a cave. The emperor walled them in and they miraculously fell into a sleep that preserved them for 187 years. A slave then broke down the wall and awoke them but the young men failed to realise how long they had been asleep. One of them went to the nearby city but could not recognise it; he spoke in an obsolete language and tried to use obsolete money and was arrested. Then the 'miracle' was revealed.

Imagine that you fall asleep in a solitary place, are presumed lost, and remain undisturbed for fifty years. Narrate your possible thoughts, feelings, and experiences as you return to a completely different world.

Unit 4

Not quite yourself: role play

Old people often imagine they are someone else; young people often wish they could get inside the mind of someone else to explore his or her thoughts and feelings; science-fiction writers sometimes write stories based on what Shakespeare in *Twelfth Night* called 'the transmigration of souls'. This was a theory of the soul passing from one human being to another, or to an animal, or to an image or from an animal to a human being and was put forward by the Greek philosopher, Pythagoras, who lived in the sixth century BC. Since then, writers have used the idea both for the content of their stories and for the angle from which the story is told: the major character in the melodramatic novel written by Oscar Wilde (in 1891) *The Picture of Dorian Grey,* the major character remains young while his picture grows old, ravaged by the sins Dorian commits until . . .! Story-tellers often assume the person of someone else in order to tell their stories — they ask the reader to believe that it is not the author telling the story himself or herself but one of the characters in the story.

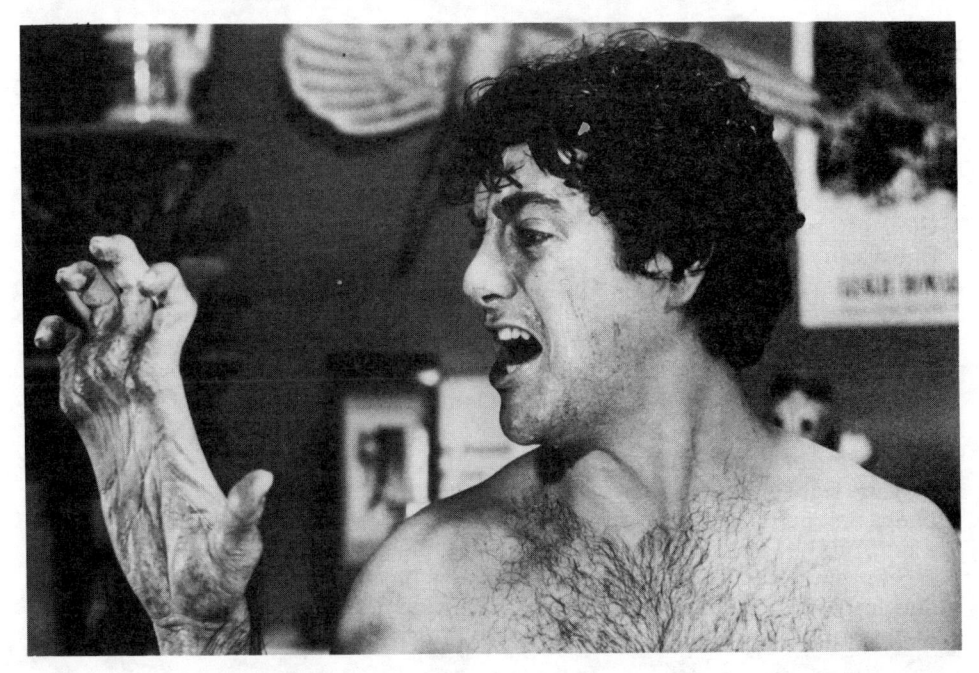

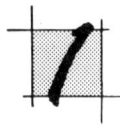

Perhaps the best-known story in which one person becomes someone else is Robert Louis Stevenson's novel *The Strange Case of Dr Jekyll and Mr Hyde* (1886). Dr Jekyll experiments to find a drug which will allow him to create a new character in which he could put all his evil instincts. Dr Jekyll becomes Mr Hyde from time to time and puts all Dr Jekyll's potential evil into practice. Mr Hyde finally commits a horrific murder and suspicion falls on Dr Jekyll, who takes his own life before he can be arrested. In a confession he leaves Dr Jekyll explains what happened to him.

I purchased at once, from a firm of wholesale chemists, a large quantity of a particular salt which I knew, from my experiments, to be the last ingredient required; and late one accursed night, I compounded the elements, watched them boil and smoke together in the glass, and when the ebullition had subsided, with a strong glow of courage, drank off the potion.

The most racking pangs succeeded, a grinding in the bones, deadly nausea, and a horror of the spirit that cannot be exceeded at the hour of birth or death. Then these agonies began swiftly to subside, and I came to myself as if out of a great sickness. There was something strange in my sensations, something indescribably new and, from its very novelty, incredibly sweet. I felt younger, lighter, happier in body . . . I stole through the corridors, a stranger to my own home; and coming to my room, I saw for the first time the appearance of Edward Hyde . . .

Robert Louis Stevenson, *The Strange Case of Dr Jekyll and Mr Hyde*

A chilling story but one which explores the human feeling of wanting to be someone else.

Here is a somewhat intriguing account, too, of someone who became someone else in real life. Read the extract carefully and then tackle one or more of the things to do which spring out of it:

One April evening in 1817 a clergyman in the village of Almondsbury, Gloucestershire, opened his cottage door to find a young woman outside. She was modestly dressed in a plain black frock with a high ruffled neck but her hair was swathed in a black turban and she babbled incoherently in a language he didn't understand.

Since she was obviously exhausted, he let her rest for a while before sending for the village overseer, who dealt with all the waifs and strays who turned up in the Parish. He too was completely baffled.

Eventually the two men bundled her into a carriage and set off for Knole Park, home of local magistrate and landowner, Samuel Worrall.

At the sight of the fine mansion the strange girl became terrified and only after a fierce struggle could she be persuaded to go inside. It was Mrs Worrall, a kind, motherly woman, who eventually managed to calm the stranger.

She was an enchanting creature, her head small and neat, her eyes black and limpid. When she smiled, her soft, full lips parted to show dazzling white teeth and, when she became excited, a rosy flush spread over her dusky skin.

Her hands were delicate and apparently unaccustomed to hard work. She appeared to be about 25 years old.

It was decided to send her, with a maid, to sleep for the night in the village inn. Supper was laid on a table, but she refused to touch it. When the landlord brought tea, however, she seized the cup greedily, covered her eyes, and gabbled some kind of prayer.

The following morning Mrs Worrall arrived at the inn to find the young woman sitting disconsolately by the fire. She jumped up, greeted her with joy, and clung to her hand possessively. There seemed no alternative but to take her back to Knole Park, where breakfast was laid. It was Good Friday and freshly baked hot cross buns were on the table. The girl reached out and took one, and then, to everyone's amazement cut off the cross and stuffed it in the bodice of her dress. Could she be a Christian?

When Mrs Worral later returned from church, she marched up to her 'guest', looked her in the eye and said, 'My good young woman, I very much fear that you are imposing on me and you can understand and answer me in my own language ...

The girl gazed back, uncomprehending.

'If so,' she went on, 'and distress has driven you to this, make a friend of me. I will give you money and clothes and put you on your journey without disclosing your conduct to anyone — but it must be on condition that you speak the truth.'

Still there was no sign of understanding.

Suddenly Mrs Worrall had a brainwave. Thumping herself on the chest, she called out, 'Worrall! Worrall!' After several repeats of this performance the girl grinned from ear to ear and, pointing to herself, shouted, 'Caraboo! Caraboo!'

For the next ten weeks Caraboo ruled the roost. The Worralls were besieged by curious friends and acquaintances, many of them bringing foreign visitors. Among them was a Portuguese from Malaya, who triumphantly announced that Caraboo was a Princess. She had been kidnapped by pirates and brought to England against her will. Her language was a mixture of dialects used on the coast of Sumatra.

Her admirers were enormously impressed. Another widely travelled friend of the Worralls, using signs, gestures, and a smattering of the words she seemed to know, finally extracted her remarkable, vividly detailed story of her capture and abduction by the pirates. Deeply impressed the Worralls settled down to living with their royal guest.

She cut the most unlikely figure on the lawns of an English country house. From a length of calico she made herself a dress with sleeves so wide and long they trailed on the ground. Her feet were bare and her head was decorated with feathers and flowers. Sometimes she carried a gong which she struck loudly and often and sometimes, armed with a bow and arrow, she would stalk about the place like Diana, goddess of the hunt.

As the weeks went by the Worralls' nerves became a little ragged. No one knew what she would do next. She liked bathing and once plunged into the lake fully dressed. She would also wash her face in the fish pond.

Then, suddenly, it was all over. One June night Caraboo stole away. She took nothing at all that did not belong to her. All her gifts and trinkets were left in a neat pile in her room. Weeks went by. After enquiries Mrs Worrall learned that her protegé had turned up in Bath and she set off in pursuit.

Hearing that Caraboo had been taken up by a fashionable society woman, Mrs Worrall burst into a tea party and found the girl surrounded by elegant admirers. When she saw Mrs Worrall she sank gracefully to her knees, begging forgiveness, saying she had run away to find someone who would help her return to her homeland. But the game was almost up. Glowing descriptions of the exotic stranger began to appear in the newspapers, including the *Bristol Journal*. A lodging-house keeper called Mrs Neale decided that the story rang a bell. Caraboo sounded very much like a fanciful young woman who had stayed with her some months before … very much like her.

Mrs Neale was eventually brought face to face with Caraboo in Mrs Worrall's presence. Without hesitation, she exclaimed, 'That's Mary Baker!' Caraboo burst into tears and admitted she was the daughter of a poor Devon cobbler and that she had never set foot in a foreign country. Caraboo was born Mary Wilcocks in the village of Witheridge, near Crediton in Devon, in 1791. Her parents were poor, respectable people with too many children. She received little education and ran wild until she was eight years old, when she was taught spinning. At 16 she was found a steady job in a farmhouse, looking after the farmer's children and doing manual work. After two years of earning ten pence a week she asked for a rise. The farmer refused and she went back home. Her father was furious and thrashed her with a leather strap; Mary ran away, lived with a group of gypsies, slept in barns, and begged for food. After being desperately ill she found a good position with Mr Matthews and his wife who lived in a handsome house. Her employer taught her to read and write, allowing her to use his library. She spent all her time devouring books that described life in far-off lands, exotic customs and romantic adventures. Later she was dismissed by Mr Matthews and fell back to being a vagabond and after many unfortunate adventures decided to become Princess Caraboo.

There were some red faces when the truth finally emerged. But people admitted she was a remarkable young woman and were curious to meet her. Linguists died to know how she had kept up the deception. Her 'language' had been made up mostly of Malay and Arabic words she had picked up from a traveller she had met in her 'vagabond' days, plus a smattering of Romany picked up from the gypsies; her knowledge of life in the East had come from books.

Mrs Worrall, once over her shock, agreed to help her Devonshire 'princess'. Mary longed to go to America. The magistrate's wife fitted her out with clothes, gave her some money, and put her on board a ship leaving Bristol. Later she developed an ardent desire to see Napoleon on his prison island of St Helena, 'borrowed' a boat and set off to see him. . . but that's another story.

Mary Baker clearly had a genius for making men believe what they wanted to believe.

M.Nicholas, *The World's Greatest Cranks and Crankpots*

1. Write an account of Mary Baker's encounter as it might have happened with Napoleon on the island of St Helena.
2. The last paragraph goes some way to accounting for Mary Baker's success. What else could you add to account for it?

3. Are you able to write a short passage in a language you invent which is consistent and carries a meaning which you can explain? (Investigate 'Esperanto' which is a widely used 'constructed' language. You may wish to do a project on the subject. Begin by looking up the name of its inventor Dr L.L. Zamenhoff in reference books in your school or public library.)

4. What other bizarre stories of deception can you find? Invent such a story of your own and write it up carefully for your English file.

5. Write a dramatic scene in which Mary's final confrontation with Mrs Worrall in Bath is shown with all its surprise, revelations, and explanations.

It is in drama, of course, that the act of one person playing or impersonating another is at the heart of things. There are those in the acting profession who believe that actors should learn their art consciously and set out by observation and skill to imitate or 'portray' the role they are playing. Another famous school of acting, the so-called 'method' school led by the Russian Stanislavski, argues that actors should 'become' the part they are playing, living and feeling the emotions and thinking the thoughts of the person on the stage.

This section of the unit explores some of the ways you can interpret, play, or become the characters in some scenes.

1. Take, for example, the following opening lines of some one-act plays. Think about the characters as they are shown, the context in which they are set, and the action that is beginning. Then develop them as you work together in groups exploring what might happen next. (Remember to remain loyal to the parts or the people represented within the circumstances shown.) Once you have developed the action and the characters you can then produce a 'script' for the play you have built up:

(*a*) *It is ten o'clock on a winter's night. The wind can be heard blowing through the dried elms outside the curtained window and its gusts occasionally buffet down the chimney in hollow moans. Mr Phillips, a man in his late forties and wearing a suit like an unmade bed, is listening to Stephen, his seventeen-year-old son. Isabel, a pretty girl with long, blonde hair, is a little younger and she is clearly afraid.*

Stephen:	I saw it as I came down the stairs, I tell you.
Mr Phillips:	Well, I'm going to take a look for myself. We can't have the whole household upset.

(*He moves towards the door, a little hesitantly, perhaps*)

Isabel:	Don't. Please, don't go out there. Stop him, Stephen.
Stephen:	Isabel's right. We'd better stay in here. There's nothing we can do.

(*b*) *The action takes place in what was once a country railway station.*

Sally:	Ben must have been out of his mind to buy this place.
Raymond:	Well, it was cheap, right in the country, and lots or room for people.

> Sally: I wish the trains *did* still come through. I could throw ham rolls at the passengers.
> Raymond: There's still one a week.

(c)   *A living-room. Mrs Baxley and Elsie are sitting at a small card table; Mrs Baxley is a woman in her forties and Elsie is a pretty but rather petulant and discontented girl of twenty or so. Elsie shuffles a pack of cards and passes them to Mrs Baxley who studies them with the air of a clairvoyant.*

> Mrs Baxley: Um ... Um ... Well, the first thing I see, Elsie, is a great surprise. Yes you're going to have a great surprise.
> Elsie: A surprise? When?
> Mrs Baxley: Very soon.
> Elsie: How soon? Next week?
> Mrs Baxley: Perhaps sooner.
> Elsie: Well it can't be much sooner. It's Sunday night and nearly next week now.
> Mrs Baxley: Well, it's coming very soon. And it isn't a nice surprise. I don't think you'll like it.

(d)   *A Victorian house is being converted into flats. Planks, ladders, paints, and building blocks are scattered about one partly converted room. Tom Reynolds, a bricklayer about fifty years old, is working on a length of partitioning. With him is Larry White, a labourer, aged about thirty.*

Suddenly there is a crash and Wally Clarkson, another labourer, enters, covered with plaster dust, and coughing.

> Tom: You all right?
> Wally: (*taking his hand from his mouth and inspecting it*): It proves I've got blood, anyway. I won't be sorry to see the last of this place. It's a death-trap.
> Larry: You did shut off the water, didn't you?
> (*The ceiling above them is bulging ominously.*)

(e)   *All the cage doors are open and the place is in a state of terrible disorder. We hear the wailing sirens of police cars. Timothy and Sarah are sitting on a bench crying. The Director of the zoo comes in followed by a police constable. The Director is a big, ruddy, irritable man.*

> Director: Is that all you can do? Sit and blubber?
> Timothy: Well, since we let them out, it'd be inconsistent to help to catch them again.
> Director: All I want to know is why! Why? (*Looking at the constable*) Constable, give these two maniacs the latest
> (*The constable pulls out a notebook and reads.*)
>
> Constable: One wombat in Tunbridge Wells; a cheetah at Headcorn; two tigers and an elephant on the A20; three wolves sighted near Ashford; gorilla heading for Canterbury. (*He looks unbelievingly from Timothy to Sarah.*) In fact, sir, (*to the Director*) the country's swarming with all sorts of ferocious animals. (*Pause.*)
> Director: Well?

2. Read the following scene and then decide:
   (*a*) how you would play one of the major characters in it;
   (*b*) how you would 'direct' it, if you were the director;
   (*c*) what set you would use for it; draw or construct the set you suggest;
   (*d*) what costumes you would use*; make drawings — coloured if you wish —
   to make your ideas clear.

(*Corder, the villain, has determined to kill Maria in case she should reveal that Corder has murdered their baby. Corder lures Maria to an old barn by saying that he would then go with her to London to be married.*)

Inside the Red Barn

Corder discovered digging a grave. (Villain's music).

Corder: All is complete; I await my victim. Will she come? Oh, yes, a woman is fool enough to do anything for the man she loves. Hark, 'tis her footstep bounding across the fields! She comes, with home in her heart, a song on her lips; little does she think that death is so near.
(*He steps into a dark corner.*)
(*Enter Maria. The music turns soft and gentle.*)

Maria: William not here? Where can he be? What ails me? A weight is at my heart as if it told some evil, and this old barn — how like a vault it looks! Fear steals upon me; I tremble in every limb. I will return to my home at once.

Corder (*advancing*): Stay, Maria!

Maria: I'm glad you are here. You don't know how frightened I have been.

Corder: Did any one see you cross the fields?

Maria: Not a soul. I remembered your instructions.

Corder: That's good. Now, Maria, do you remember a few days ago threatening to betray me about the child to Constable Ayres?   (*Tremolo fiddles*)

Maria: A girlish threat made in a heat of temper, because you refused to do justice to one you had wronged so greatly. Do not speak of that now. Let us leave this place.

Corder: Not yet, Maria. You don't think my life is to be held at the bidding of a silly girl. *No*, look what I have made here!
    (*He draws her to the grave. Slow music.*)

Maria: A grave. Oh William, what do you mean?

Corder: To kill you, bury your body there. You are a clog upon my actions, a chain that keeps me from reaching ambitious heights. You are to die.

Maria (*kneels*): But not by your hand, the hand that I have clasped in love and confidence. Oh! think, William, how much I have sacrificed for you; think of our little child above, now in heaven, pleads for its mother's life. Oh spare, oh spare me!

Corder: 'Tis useless; my mind's resolved. You die tonight.
    (*Thunder and lightning.*)

---

* In the original play by T. W. Robertson, *Maria Marten or The Murder in the Red Barn*, Maria arrives disguised as a boy, but you may, if you wish, dress her in feminine costume.

Maria: Wretch! Since neither prayers nor tears will touch your
          strong heart, Heaven will surely nerve my arm to battle
          for my life.   (*She seizes Corder.*)
Corder: Foolish girl, desist!
Maria: Never with life!
Maria (*soft music*)*:* William, I am dying. Your cruel hand has
          stilled the heart that beat in love alone for thee. Think
          not to escape the hand of justice, for when least
          expected it will mark you down; at that moment think of
          Maria's wrongs. Death claims me, and with my last
          breath I die blessing and forgiving thee.   (*Dies*)
Corder: Blessing and forgiveness! And for me, her (*Loud music*)
          murderer! What have I done! Oh Maria, awake, awake;
          do not look so tenderly upon me! Let indignation
          lighten from your eyes and blast me!
          Oh may this crime for ever stand accurst, the last of
          murders as it is the worst.

3. Several of Shakespeare's plays, amongst others, complicate the role-playing
   in drama even further. The characters on the stage play somebody else in
   disguise and this leads to some extraordinary complications in the plots—
   women falling in love with other women dressed as boys; a king dressed as a
   common soldier moving amongst his troops unrecognised before a major
   battle; a country bumpkin transformed into a creature with an ass's head....
   Look up some of the following scenes in a book of Shakespeare's plays and
   decide how you would direct or play in them. All the references are to the
   Oxford edition of *The Complete Works of William Shakespeare*, but it is better
   to look up the scenes you choose in one of the New Arden editions of the plays
   if you can find them in your public library. These editions give you very full
   notes on the texts:

(*a*) *Twelfth Night*: Act III, scene 1, where Viola is disguised as a boy.

(*b*) *Henry V*:   Act IV, scene 1, where King Henry moves in disguise
                   amongst his soldiers before the battle of Agincourt.

(*c*) *King Lear*:   *Act IV, scene 1, where Edgar, hunted by the authorities who
                   suspect him of a plot, returns to help his father by using the
                   disguise of a madman.*

(*d*) *The Merry Wives of Windsor*:
                   Act IV, scene 2, where the huge Sir John Falstaff tries to
                   escape from a jealous husband by disguising himself
                   (somewhat grotesquely, as it turns out) as a woman.

(*e*) *The Merchant of Venice*:
                   Act IV, scene 1, where Portia dresses as a male doctor of laws
                   and Nerissa, her maid, is dressed as a lawyer's clerk to
                   defend Antonio in court against the grasping Shylock.

You may wish to try to write your own short play in which one or more of
the characters is in disguise. (Films also use the technique, too. Many of
the adventures of Robin Hood in his fight against the wicked sheriff of

Nottingham showed the hero in a variety of disguises, usually that of a friar or of a woman!)

4. The art of acting or of directing depends on the skill of interpretation; similarly the great set-designers (e.g. Gordon Craig) need the imagination to convey the meaning they see in a play to an audience's imagination. All need to move towards the conception of the play that the writer had at the time when it was written.

Take a play you know well — one you are studying perhaps at the moment — and discuss with your English group:

(a) the different interpretations you could give the major character in the light of the text itself. Remember that some of the major directors insist that actors study the text of the play with its background and period before the work on the production itself actually gets under way. You should be able to justify your interpretation of the character from what he or she says, what he or she does, and what others in the play say about him or her;

(b) the essential meaning of the play that you would wish as a director to communicate to an audience. Ask yourself questions such as 'What does the play mean?' 'Can the plot and the characters be taken merely at face-value or is there another level of interpretation possible?', 'How can we find out what the playwright intended?' (Samuel Beckett's *Waiting for Godot* is an excellent example of a play which has attracted a number of interpretations!);

(c) what set would be appropriate for the meaning(s) of the play? Should it be realistic, symbolic, or traditional? How will the play be represented in the production? On a stage with a proscenium arch? As 'theatre-in-the-round'? What lighting will there be? How will the set fit in with the costumes?

Try to sketch some of your ideas in the field of visual presentation of the play.

5. Improvise from a scene in a play you are studying as a way of arriving at an interpretation of a character. Joan Littlewood in her theatre at Stratford in East London used to encourage actors to do this as an essential part of the work of the production; in this way the actors could play the role of someone else authentically, because they knew what the character would feel, think, and do in a situation.

 Role-playing, or becoming someone else, is also an art that the writers of fiction use in order to tell their stories. It is, of course, part of the skill of directed writing.

Any act where language is used presupposes *four* things:

(a) a speaker or writer;
(b) a topic (the subject matter);
(c) a context (the situation in which the language is being used);
(d) a listener or a reader (the audience).

The language needs to be appropriate to all of these four areas.

The writer's or speaker's point of view is essentially the position from which the writer or speaker is using the language. This position may be that of the writer or speaker now or in the past, or it may be the position that he or she takes up as a role. The skill of the satirist, 'the demolition expert', as Kenneth Tynan once described George Bernard Shaw, is to seem to be writing from one position when in fact he or she is writing from another.

Now try some of these exercises to show your skill in using language from your own point of view or adopting a role other than that of yourself in producing either a piece of spoken or written English or using signs of another kind:

1. With the help of a map, explain to a potential visitor to your school or college how to reach the head's office from the main entrance.
2. With the help of the following comparative chart describe in the form of a summary the differences for Los Angeles in their presentation of the Olympic Games in 1932 and in 1944. (Your own description should have a particular audience at which it is aimed — newspaper or sports-journal readers or listeners to a broadcast about the Olympic Games to be held in 1989.)

OLYMPIC CITY THEN AND NOW

Los Angeles is one of three cities (with London and Paris) that have twice hosted modern Olympic Games. Things — apart from fame — were different then

	1932	1984
Population	1,283,000	2,979,480 (1981)
City Budget	$37.7 million (1932-33)	$1,732.7 million
Tallest Building	City Hall 27 storeys	First Interstate Bank 62 storeys
Average number of Employees in Movie Industry	290,000	223,000
Number of Air Passengers	84,460 (1937), Glendale/ Burbank Airport	32.7 million, Los Angeles International Airport
Road Mileage	4,912 miles	6,447 miles (1980)
Number of Automobiles	772,399 (county)	4,044,000 (county)
Number of Broadcasting Stations Radio Television	16 (1935) 0	71 19
Funding of Olympic Games	Issued $1 million public bond	Budgeted $472 million; sponsored by large private corporations

3. Listen to tonight's main news bulletins on *one* of the BBC television channels and on *one* of the Independent television channels:
   (*a*) make a list of news items included on both channels;
   (*b*) make a list of news items included on one channel but not on the other;
   (*c*) try to describe any significant 'slanting' of the news you spotted on both channels;
   (*d*) produce a short explanation of how the personality of the newscaster affected your response to the news item.
4. Prepare a speech to be delivered by someone (not necessarily yourself) interested in scientific research to a group of ecology or conservation enthusiasts on the subject of, 'The need to carry out experiments on animals'.
5. Invent some signs or notices (which use no words) to indicate the following to the public:
   (*a*) toads crossing the road ahead;
   (*b*) no entry for elephants;
   (*c*) women only — no men allowed;
   (*d*) silence!;
   (*e*) make enquiries at the reception desk;
   (*f*) keep to the path;
   (*g*) office closed;
   (*h*) pet-owners allowed only if accompanied by pets;
   (*i*) school closed — teachers on strike;
   (*j*) no running!

Finally, a poem by Dannie Abse. It talks of the loss of personal identity, assumed masks that people wear, and the search again for oneself in a world that won't allow you to be yourself.

THE TRIAL

The heads around the table disagree,
some say hang him from the gallows tree.

Some say high and some say low
to swing, swing, swing, when the free winds blow.

I wanted to be myself, no more,
so I screwed off the face that I always wore.

I pulled out the nails one by one —
I'd have given that face to anyone.

For these vile features were hardly mine;
to wear another's face is a spiritual crime.

Why, imagine the night when I would wed
to kiss with wrong lips in the bridal bed...

But now the crowd screams loud in mockery:
oh, string him up from the gallows tree.

Silence, the Judge commands, or I'll clear the Court,
to hang a man up is not a sport—

though some say high and some say low
to swing, swing, swing, when the free winds blow.

Prisoner, allow me once more to ask:
what did you do with your own pure mask?

I told you, your honour, I threw it away,
it was only made of skin-coloured clay.

A face is a man, a bald juryman cries,
for one face lost, another man dies.

Gentlemen, this citizen we daren't acquit
until we know what he did with it.

It was only a face, your honour, that I lost;
how much can such a sad thing cost?

A mask is a lifetime, my bad man,
to replace such a gift nobody can.

Consider the case of that jovial swan
who took a god's face off to put a bird's face on,

and Leda swooning by the side of the sea
and the swan's eyes closed in lechery.

No! No, your honour, my aim was just—
I did what every true man must.

Quiet prisoner! Why I remember a priest remark
that he picked up a dog's face in the dark.

Then he got as drunk as a man can be
and barked at God in blasphemy.

But it was a human face, sir, I cast away;
for that offence do I have to pay?

The heads around the table disagree,
some say hang him from the gallows tree.

Some say high and some say low
to swing, swing, swing, when the free winds blow.

At the back of the courtroom quietly stand
his father and mother hand in hand.

They can't understand the point of this case
or why he discarded his own dear face.

But it's not *my* face, father, he had said,
I don't want to die in a strange wrong bed.

Look in the mirror, mother, stare in deep;
is that mask your own, yours to keep?

The mirror is oblong, the clock is round,
all our wax faces go underground.

Once I built a bridge right into myself
to ransack my soul for invisible wealth

and afterwards I tore off my mask because
I found not the person I thought I was.

With the wrong mask, another man's life I live —
I must seek my own face, find my own grave.

The heads around the table disagree,
some say hang him from the gallows tree.

I'll sum up, the severe Judge moans,
showing the white of his knucklebones.

What is a face but the thing that you see
the symbol and fate of identity?

How would we recognise each from each:
a dog from a man — which face on a leash?

And when the tears fall where no face is,
will the tears be mine or will they be his?

To select hot coal or gold no man is free —
each choice being determined by identity.

But exchange your face, then what you choose
is gained like love by what you lose.

Now you twelve jurymen please retire,
put your right hand in ice and your left in fire.

A hole where the face was frightens us
and a man who can choose is dangerous.

So what is your verdict going to be,
should he be hung from the gallows tree?

Oh, some say high and some say low
to swing, swing, swing, when the free winds blow.

Daniel Abse

1. What kind of face do the following people see you are wearing when they look at you?
   (*a*) your parents;   (*c*) your teachers;
   (*b*) your friends;   (*d*) yourself.
2. If you could change yourself and take up another kind of mask, what sort of person would you like to be?
3. Write a short account of how hard you find it to be yourself in a life where others assume you are one person and you know yourself to be quite different. Is is possible to play two different roles? 'What is your **verdict** going to be?'

Unit 5

Work:
becoming a sorcerer's apprentice

The world of work is one that school-leavers face with reluctance or with enthusiasm or with complacency — but it is one that they always face with uncertainty and even with difficulty.

This unit sets out to explore some of the emotions and attitudes associated with the world of work and to encourage you to use your language skills to write and to talk about your own feelings and ideas.

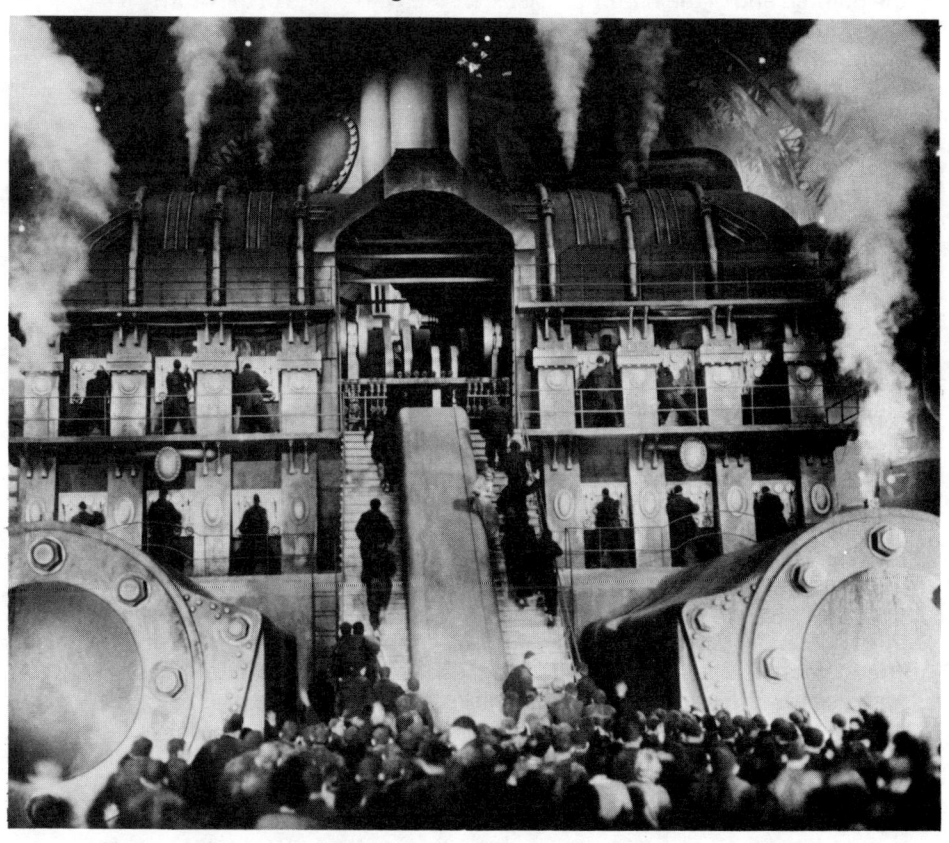

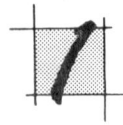

First, here are two passages which describe how two young people, sensitive and alert, faced this strange new world. Compare them and then answer the questions which follow. One set is in the form of multiple-choice questions which require you to think about possibilities and to choose the correct answer and the other set is in the form of more traditional open-ended questions used by some GCSE boards.

(*a*) At fifteen, half my friends left school to get themselves into apprenticeships. I stuck it out for another couple of years into the sixth form, and then I dropped out into a trade and onto a building site. It was a switch from calculus, the theory of valency and the principle of the
5   conservation of energy to the medieval overtones of the deeds of apprenticeship. But I learnt a trick or two.
    My first job was to brew tea. Then a tall plasterer named Alf Smith, who looked like a local version of Lee Marvin, handed me an empty putty-drum and a spike-headed hammer and told me to make a brazier and get a
10   coke fire going. I took the putty-drum outside and nipped into the next house to examine their brazier. It was perfectly round with a regular series of holes punched in it. Large at the bottom and small at the top. I marched back to my unblemished drum and gave it sharp belt in the middle with the pointed end of the hammer. Disaster: the whole side of the drum
15   caved in and there was only one microscopic puncture in the metal. I tried to straighten the side back into shape by forcing my foot into the drum. Gradually I prised down on the indentation — and my foot shot through the bottom. Immediately the metal sprang back, trapping my leg. I couldn't force it apart with my hands so I clomped across the road and
20   forced the handle of a spade into the drum and withdrew my leg. It was bleeding.
    Next I grabbed a spar about six-foot long, wedged the drum under the wheel of a concrete mixer and began levering the crumpled side into shape. Then suddenly the opposite side of the drum collapsed and I
25   landed on my back in a puddle. By this time I was fighting mad and hammered blow after blow on the drum. It wilted, warped, and flattened. It was only then that I realised I had an audience: the new gang of plasterers had been watching the performance from the sanctuary of the houses. Some of them were almost speechless with laughter. I was so
30   angry I felt I could burst. Alf Smith came loping out of the house with a new putty-drum. 'That was a technical piece of artistry if ever I saw it,' he said. He took me across to where the sand was stored and carefully filled the drum with sand. Then, with a series of light taps with the hammer, he punched a neat line of holes in the side of the drum, without a fraction of
35   distortion. As I carried the completed brazier back to the house, Alf asked me if I knew the difference between a wise man and a fool. 'A wise man knows what he doesn't know and a fool doesn't. And you can tell a wise man because he'll ask when he doesn't know and a fool won't. OK?'
    When the gang was working on ceilings, the most junior apprentice —
40   namely, me — would mix the plaster, move the scaffolds, and work on the trowel when the plaster began its final set. The plaster used on the ceilings was specially treated to set slowly. I'd take half a bucket of water to where the plaster was stored, fill it to the brim with powder and leave it to soak for

a couple of minutes. Then I'd beat it to a fine cream with a mixing stick.
45 After a couple of months I'd learnt a few dodges. I found out that a bucket mixed with dirty water or with a handful of dust thrown in would set very quickly. On the other hand, a couple of cups of cold tea could delay the set for hours. Once I'd discovered this, the craftsmen I was working with only crossed me at their peril. Three quick fast-setting buckets of plaster would
50 have them galloping frantically round the scaffold. A few slow-setting buckets kept them at a ceiling long after everyone else had gone home.

At school you used words and ideas and numbers: 'things went on in the front of your mind' is the best way I can express it. It was different serving an apprenticeship. You had to upgrade the way that your senses
55 worked. Walking across a ceiling scaffold, you were constantly sensing the position and the spring of the planks without looking down. Apprenticeship wasn't about this business of being bound to a master; it was about developing co-ordination, the ability to move materials without effort, and developing a sense of space.
60 I've talked to training managers in recent years who believe that the apprenticeship system should be scrapped. But I'm not sure whether this is right for jobs that demand muscular strength, agility and staying power. From the age of fifteen to twenty, a person can develop an optimum muscle structure in relation to his job. And in the long run surely this
65 makes the job easier for him. For me, it shouldn't have been a liberation from school — but it was. It shouldn't have been the most vital part of my education — but it was.

Bob Houlton, 'My Apprenticeship', *The Listener*

1 At school in the sixth form the writer studied mainly
   A computers
   B science
   C ecology
   D history
   E biology

2 The writer was probably asked to brew the tea for the plasterers because they
   A wanted him to learn his place
   B tried to keep him busy
   C had no other work for him
   D gave the job traditionally to juniors
   E wanted to break him in gradually

3 He nipped into the next house to examine the brazier to find out
   A how the holes were arranged
   B if their putty-drum was like his
   C how to carry out the job
   D if someone could help him
   E how the putty-drum would be used

4 The holes in the putty-drum (lines 11–4) were bigger at the bottom than at the top in order to
   A make a symmetrical pattern
   B give the drum better stability

   C let the heat out more quickly
   D keep the drum's strength when hot
   E allow for a good draught

5 The 'disaster' (line 14) that occurred with the first blow of the hammer was that the
   A hammer did not work
   B drum split down one side
   C hole made was too small
   D drum's side sprang out of shape
   E metal proved much too strong

6 'Microscopic' (line 15) means that the hole he had made was
   A uneven in shape
   B impossible to find
   C out of position
   D impossible to repair
   E hard to see

7 Which one of the following words is closest in meaning to 'prised' as used in line 17?
   A Forced
   B Stamped
   C Levered
   D Kicked
   E Hammered

8 'Clomped' (line 19) suggests mainly that his walk across the road was
   A ridiculous
   B clumsy
   C embarrassing
   D painful
   E determined

9 The writer was 'fighting mad' (line 25) most probably because he
   A was frustrated at not being able to do the job
   B thought the plasterers were laughing at him
   C had hurt his leg which was bleeding
   D realised the men had played a joke on him
   E believed that he had to exert more force

10 'Wilted, warped, and flattened' (line 26) suggests that the final appearance of the drum was all the following EXCEPT
   A twisted
   B jagged
   C bent
   D dented
   E squashed

11 'Performance' (line 28) suggests that the actions of the writer had been
  A enjoyed by those watching his antics
  B planned in advance by the plasterers
  C exaggerated to entertain his spectators
  D met with laughter from an audience
  E intensified because he had become angry

12 The houses provided 'sanctuary' (line 28) for the plasterers because they were
  A sheltered
  B uninvolved
  C safe
  D undisturbed
  E hidden

13 As Alf Smith appeared with the new putty-drum (line 29) he
  A was speechless with laughter
  B took long, careless strides
  C made everything seem easy
  D limped because of its weight
  E felt embarrassed for the apprentice

14 When Alf Smith said, 'That was a technical piece of artistry if ever I saw it' (line 31) he was being
  A clever
  B truthful
  C complimentary
  D helpful
  E sarcastic

15 Alf Smith's distinction between a wise man and a fool (lines 26–7) depends on the facts that a wise man
        1 needs everything explained to him
        2 recognises his own ignorance
        3 works out solutions for himself
        4 asks others who know for help
  A 1 and 2 only
  B 1 and 3 only
  C 2 and 3 only
  D 2 and 4 only
  E 3 and 4 only

16 The youngest member of the team of plasterers was expected to do all the following EXCEPT
  A erect the scaffolds
  B prepare the plasterer
  C make the tea

D clean the tools
E light the fire

17 All the following were steps in the preparation of properly mixed plaster
EXCEPT
  A adding the plaster to the water very quickly
  B stirring the mixture with a clean stick
  C waiting for the plaster to absorb the water
  D using half a bucket of water to a bucket of plaster
  E mixing the plaster and the water to a fine consistency

18 The writer found that the difference between being at school and being an
apprentice lay mainly in the fact that at school it was more a matter of
  A obeying rules
  B understanding theory
  C gaining practical experience
  D solving problems
  E learning by mistakes

19 The writer concluded that on balance he favoured an apprenticeship system
for some trades because it
  A came at a time when muscular co-ordination was easily learnt
  B gave a sense of liberation to the school-leaver
  C offered work-experience to those looking for work
  D ensured a through grounding for a particular trade
  E allowed young people to expand their knowledge cheaply

20 The last two sentences suggest all the following EXCEPT
that Bob Houlton
  A felt he was better than others in manual jobs
  B thought some aspects of school were insufficient
  C learnt much from his apprenticeship early in life
  D derived some benefit from staying on at school
  E recognised the value of apprenticeship in his personal development

(*b*) The second passage is from the second part of Maxim Gorky's
autobiography. He was obliged to work for a living from the age eight but read
voraciously and educated himself. He supported the Russian Revolution very
strongly and by the time he died at the age of 68 in 1936 his reputation as a writer
was well acknowledged.

And so my apprenticeship began, as a shop-boy in a 'fashionable' shoe shop
in the high street. The owner was a small, fattish man with a swarthy, tired
face, green teeth, and eyes the colour of muddy water. He looked as if he was
blind and I made funny faces at him to see if he really was.
  'Stop screwing your face up,' he would say in a soft, but menacing, voice.
  It was very nasty to think that those bleary eyes could actually see me and, I
just did not believe it. Perhaps he was only *guessing* that I was pulling faces?

'I said stop screwing your face up,' he repeated — this time in an even softer voice. As he spoke his blubbery lips barely parted. Then I heard that rasping, whispering voice again:

'And don't scratch your arms! You're in a high-class shop now, in the high street, so don't forget it! Boys should stand by the door, still as statchers...'

I did not know what a 'statcher' was and I could not stop scratching. Both my arms were covered up to the elbows with red patches and sores: those itch-mites were eating away at me and I could hardly bear the pain.

'What were you doing back home?' he asked as he inspected my arms.

When I told him he shook his round head, which was covered with grey hair plastered with oil, and he started showering me with insults:

'Scavenging — that's worse than begging — or stealing even.'

I proudly announced: 'Oh, I used to steal as well!'

At this he planted his hands on the counter like a cat, looked at me with his frightened empty eyes and hissed right into my face:

'Wha-at? Who put you up to that?'

'Look, I won't say any more about it now. But if I catch you stealing shoes or money from *my* shop I'll have you put away until you come of age!' The way he said this, in that calm voice of his, was even more frightening, and I began to dislike him more and more.

Besides the owner, my cousin Sasha helped to sell shoes, and there was a slimy, red-faced smart aleck of a senior assistant. Sasha wore a reddish frock-coat, a starched shirt-front, a tie, and trousers with turn-ups. He was very snooty and almost completely ignored me. When Grandfather brought me to my new master and asked Sasha to teach me the trade, Sasha frowned solemnly and issued the following warning.

'Now he'll have to do what *I* tell him!'

Grandfather made me bow to him by pressing my head down hard.

'Listen to Sasha,' he said. 'He's older than you and knows all about the shoe trade.'

Sasha's eyes rolled as he too tried to impress this on me:

'Yes! don't you forget what Grandfather's just told you.'

From the very first day he did all he could to take advantage of his seniority. Once the shop-owner had to tell him:

'Kashirin, stop goggling!'

'Me? But I wasn't, sir,' Sasha replied, lowering his head. But my new master wouldn't leave him alone:

'And don't keep lowering your head. The customers will think you're a goat!'

The senior assistant laughed obsequiously and the owner's mouth spread out into an ugly grin. Sasha turned purple and hid behind the counter...

When a lady came into the shop the proprietor would take his hand out of his pocket, smooth his whiskers and plaster his face with an oily smile. But his empty eyes never moved. The senior assistant would stiffen up, draw his elbows in to his sides and let his wrists dangle respectfully. Sasha would blink in a frightened sort of way as though he were trying to hide his bulging eyes. I would stand by the door, scratching my arms so that no one could see me, surveying the whole ceremony. Then the senior assistant would kneel at the lady's feet and start trying shoes on. He could spread his fingers out astonishingly wide and his hands would start trembling. He was so careful when he touched a lady's foot that it seemed he was scared of hurting it. But most of the ladies' feet were fat and shaped like bottles with tapering necks, pointing downwards. Once a lady jerked her foot away, wriggled, and exclaimed: 'Oo, you're tickling!…'

'I was just trying to be polite, madam,' the assistant explained quickly.

It was highly amusing to see him crawling round the ladies and I often had to stare out into the street to stop laughing. But I normally found it absolutely impossible to keep my eyes off what was going on and the assistant's movements were really very funny…

Life was hard and boring most of the time in that shop. I began to see the seamy, deceitful side of life. Very often a lady customer would leave without buying a thing and then the owner, the senior assistant, and Sasha would feel insulted. The owner would wipe the smile off his face, stuff it in his pocket and start ordering me around.

'Kashirin, put the shoes away!'

Then he would start swearing again.

'Old bag! Sticking her ugly mug in here. The silly old bitch must have got fed up sitting at home. She's got nothing better to do than hang round the shops all day. If she were my wife, *I'd* show her…'

Maxim Gorky, *My Apprenticeship* (1915)

1. Both passages deal with apprenticeships but in what major respects do they differ?

2. Describe orally or in writing the major characteristics of *either* (*a*) the owner, (*b*) the senior assistant, *or* (*c*) Sasha. (Back up your descriptions with examples taken from the passage.)

3. What picture do you get of the writer himself from the passage?

4. Write a description of the owner of a shop you know well or of one of the shop-assistants working there.

5. Recount some of your own experiences *either* as a shopper *or* a shop-assistant, doing perhaps a Saturday job.

6. Devise and improvise a one-act play on the subject of an amusing incident you observed in a shop.

7. What are your own thoughts about an apprenticeship scheme? Do you think it is a useful way of learning a trade or is it merely a way of exploiting cheap labour?

8. Write down or discuss your views about more recent attempts to give young people work experience.

9. Attempt to re-write the account of incidents given in the first passage using a style and point of view closer to that of the writer of the second passage. (This is a difficult exercise but one which will demand a careful analysis of what both passages consist.) *Alternatively*, try to re-write the account of incidents given in the second passage using a style and point of view closer to that of the writer of the first passage.

10. Both these passages contain an implied criticism of older people responsible for operating apprenticeship schemes. Try to make a summary of what these implied criticisms are.

A microbiologist and a member of Oxford City Council was reported in *The Times* of 3 August 1985 to have advised the young employed to 'eat porridge, pick berries off bushes, buy second-hand clothes at jumble sales'. The problem of unemployment amongst school-leavers and others was enormous in 1984 and 1985. The following is an article, also from *The Times*, summarising the position as David Smith, the paper's economic correspondent saw it.

Jobless queue growth declining

By David Smith, Economics Correspondent

Unemployment, which has been grinding steadily upwards for six years, may now be steadying. Figures released this week, while showing a 6,500 increase in the adult jobless total last month, suggest a marked slowdown in the extent to which the dole queues are lengthening.

When the jobs measures announced in the Budget last March start to take effect, including 100,000 extra places on the Community Programme, and changes in national insurance contributions from October 1, unemployment may stop rising and even head slowly downwards.

In the latest three months, adult unemployment fell by an average of 300 a month, mainly because of the unexpected 8,100 drop in the jobless total in June. These were the best figures for any three months since late 1979.

Job vacancies, while still only a fraction of the number of people available for work, have risen in vacancies to 179,700 last month, after seasonal adjustment, and vacancies were at their highest level for five years.

Most vacancies are not notified to Jobcentres, and Whitehall officials believe the total vacancies in the economy are probably between 475,000 and 575,000.

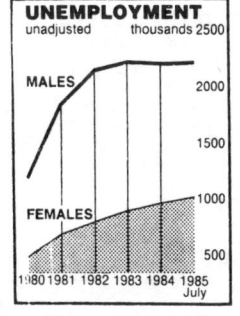

UNEMPLOYMENT
unadjusted   thousands 2500

Even so, with unemployment standing at 3,175,400 for adults and 3,235,036 including claimant school leavers (there are another 134,455 summer school leavers who will not enter the jobless total until they become eligible for benefit next month), the problem is a huge one. Alongside totals such as those, vacancies are dwarfed.

So what is happening to unemployment now? The improved outlook for the next few months rests on two factors. First, the economic recovery is now in its fifth year, having begun in the spring of 1981. For the initial phase of the recovery, output rose but employment was unchanged or fell while unemployment

continued to rise because of an increase in the labour force.

In the past two years, employment has increased and, in spite of a fast growing labour force, this is beginning to tell on the unemployment totals.

The second factor is that, in the approach to the last Budget, the Government began to fear that unemployment was not going to fall of its own accord. Mr Nigel Lawson, Chancellor of the Exchequer, introduced his "Budget for Jobs" with the emphasis split between new job creation measures – including the 100,000 extra Community Programme places and a doubling of time spent on the Youth Training Scheme from one to two years – together with policy changes designed to

boost the demand for labour by private sector employers.

National insurance contributions for low-paid workers will be reduced from October 1 with the intention of encouraging companies to take on more people. At the end of last month, the Government announced that wages council provisions will no longer apply to about half a million workers under the age of 21, again with the aim of freeing the labour market and boosting employment.

The rosier outlook during next year is based on the combination of a mature phase in the economic recovery with the maximum impact of extra government job-creation measures. Unemployment is quite likely to edge downwards.

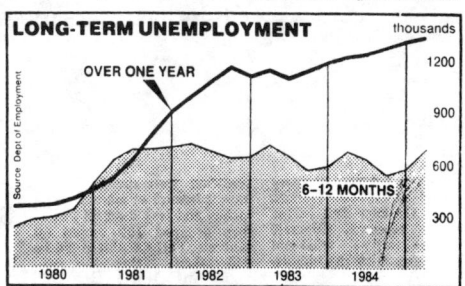

LONG-TERM UNEMPLOYMENT   thousands

OVER ONE YEAR

6–12 MONTHS

Source: Dept of Employment

1980   1981   1982   1983   1984

1200
900
600
300

1. Using the facts, rather than the opinions, expressed in this article write the responses on unemployment given by two candidates at a parliamentary by-election to the question, 'What are your views about the unemployment situation in the country?' (Make it clear from what is said what party each of the candidates you choose belongs to.)

2. With the help of some of the facts and figures given here design and write an article on unemployment for a national daily newspaper whose style and attitude you are very familiar with.

3. (*a*) Write a letter intended to be published in *The Times* (or in another daily paper if you wish) protesting about phrases such as 'improved outlook', 'rosier outlook', and 'fast-growing labour force' the article contains, from the point of view of a long-term unemployed man or woman.

(b) Write the response, too, of the editor of the newspaper defending the article from such an attack.

4. The article as it stands, realistic as it is, ends on an optimistic note. It contains phrases, too, which reinforce its overall optimistic attitude. Are you able to use the details to produce an article which, although still realistic, reflects a more pessimistic attitude?

5. What are your reactions as a young person about to enter the employment market to such an article?

6. What are your own aims in employment once you leave school? What satisfaction do you think work will give you?

 Here are three poems about work. How far do they reflect your own thoughts and feelings?

WORK

(a) There is no point in work
unless it absorbs you
like an absorbing game.

If it doesn't absorb you
if it's never any fun,
don't do it.

When a man goes out into his work
he is alive like a tree in spring,
he is living, not merely working.

D. H. Lawrence

(b)   TOADS REVISITED
Walking around in the park
Should feel better than work:
The lake, the sunshine,
The grass to lie on,

Blurred playground noises
Beyond black-stockinged nurses—
Not a bad place to be
Yet it doesn't suit me.

Being one of the men
You meet of an afternoon:
Palsied old step-takers,
Hare-eyed clerks with the jitters,

Waxed-flesh out-patients
Still vague from accidents,
And characters in long coats
Deep in the litter baskets—

All dodging the toad work
By being stupid or weak.
Think of being them!
Hearing the hours chime,

Watching the bread delivered,
The sun by clouds covered,
The children going home;
Think of being them,

Turning over their failures
By some bed of lobelias,
Nowhere to go but indoors,
No friends but empty chairs—

No, give me my in-tray,
My loaf-haired secretary,
My shall-I-keep-the-call-in-Sir:
What else can I answer,

When the lights come on at four
At the end of another year?
Give me your arm, old toad;
Help me down Cemetery Road.

Philip Larkin

(c)

TOADS

Why should I let the toad *work*
　Squat on my life?
Can't I use my wits as a pitchfork
　And drive the brute off?

Six days of the week it soils
　With its sickening poison—
Just for paying a few bills!
　That's out of proportion.

Lots of folk live on their wits:
　Lecturers, lispers,
Losels*, loblolly† men, louts—
　They don't end as paupers;

Lots of folk live up lanes
　With fires in a bucket,
Eat windfalls and tinned sardines—
　They seem to like it.

Their nippers have got bare feet,
　Their unspeakable wives
Are skinny as whippets — and yet
　No one actually *starves*.

* Good-for-nothings. † A dialect word for louts.

Ah, were I courageous enough
　　To shout, *Stuff your pension*!
But I know, all too well, that's the stuff
　　That dreams are made on:

For something sufficiently toad-like
　　Squats in me too;
Its hunkers‡ are heavy as hard luck,
　　And cold as snow,

And will never allow me to blarney
　　My way to getting
The fame and the girl and the money
　　All at one sitting.

　I don't say, one bodies the other
　　One's spiritual truth;
But I do say it's hard to lose either,
　　When you have both.

Philip Larkin

1. What commentary about society today can you find in all these poems?
2. How does Lawrence's attitude to work differ from Larkin's? Explain how your own attitude is closer to one rather than the other or how it differs from both.
3. Write your own poem or piece of prose which has at its heart an image for work which you explore (just as Larkin used the image of a 'toad').

 Use one of the following quotations from literature as a springboard into your own piece of creative writing which may be a poem, a story, a piece of prose, a short play, or some other kind of composition:

(*a*) 'Work is the curse of the drinking classes.'

(H. Pearson, *Life of Oscar Wilde*, 1946)

(*b*) It's no go the picture palace, it's no go the stadium,
　　It's no go the country cot with a pot of pink geraniums,
　　It's no go the Government grants, it's no go the elections,
　　Sit on your arse for fifty years and hang your hat on a pension.

　　It's no go my honey, love, it's no go my poppet;
　　Work your hands from day to day, the winds will blow the profit.
　　The glass is falling hour by hour, the glass will fall for ever,
　　But if you break the bloody glass, you won't hold up the weather.

(Louis Macneice)

(*c*) Term, holidays, term, holidays till we leave school,
　　and then work, work, work till we die.

(C.S. Lewis)

‡Conservative people.

(*d*) If any would not work, neither should he eat.

(*The Bible*, 2 Thessalonians, iii, 10)

(*e*) No man is born into the world, whose work
Is not born with him; there is always work,
And tools to work withal, for those who will.

(J.R. Lowell, *A Glance behind the Curtain*)

The two pictures below and on page 82 show two groups of people at work. Use *one* of them as the basis for a piece of descriptive writing to include in your English file. (Both paintings are full of detail and are well composed; give to your work an equally sound 'composition' and sense of detail.)

Unit 6

Humour

'A funny thing happened to me on the way to . . .'

It is not easy to be funny. Some of the most famous comics and comedians declare that theirs is a hard profession. The whole area of humour is bedevilled by the fact that what one person finds funny another may find deadly serious. Everyone who has tried to tell a joke and lost the way will realise what an art humour is. George Orwell may have overstated the seriousness of humour when he said, 'Whatever is funny is subversive; every joke is ultimately a custard pie' but there is an element of truth in his remark.

This unit is not about jokes, however; it *is* about the skill that writers and speakers have shown in making other people laugh.

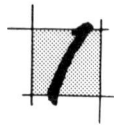 Let us begin in school with a history lesson at Stonehill Street School, where Edmund Blishen was once a teacher:

One morning I was talking about the work of the archaeologists. I wanted to show how delicate it could be and so told a story of Sir Leonard Woolley digging out a statue with a teaspoon.

Bubbles of giggling rose from the spot where Johnny had been sitting. He had sunk under his desk, so disrupted by amusement that he wasn't able even to maintain a sitting position.

'Oh, forget about him, sir,' said the class. Johnny's weakness was unpopular with them. They felt that he went too far.

'Go on, sir,' said a boy.

But the bubbles rising from Johnny' desk were beginning to pop, explosions of hilarity that made it impossible to go on talking.

'I'll deal with him, sir,' said Toll, a grim boy with no sense of humour at all. He crossed to Johnny's desk and contemplated the writhing victim of comic hysteria on the floor.

'Get up, Richards!' he commanded.

More boys sprang to their feet.

'You hold his head. Grab his legs! Come on, Richards! Sit up! Sir's waiting! What's so funny? Come on!' They were harsh with disgust.

'Look, Richards,' I said incautiously, 'a teaspoon…'

The little body, that had been on the point of submitting to its manhandling, winced and quivered to pieces again.

'Come on, some more of you!' they shouted. 'Get his arms! Hold his arms tight! Ouch! Keep your legs still, Richards! Come on, sir! Give a hand!'

Then their wrath was doubled.

'Sir's grinning! Sir thinks it funny! Come on, sir!' It's not a joke! You oughtn't allow it! Ouch! You kick me again, Richards…'

There was nothing I could do. With Johnny's collapse I had seen the vision he must have seen. Sir Leonard Woolley, in Johnny's eyes a grave aristocrat, solemnly uniformed, kneeling in the sand, a look of unutterable learnedness on his face, and in his hand a teaspoon. Digging, as though at a monstrous gutty ice-cream, he placed each spoonful in his mouth, his eyes enlarging with approval. And bit by bit the statue rose before him, its ancient gaze wide as it beheld its rescuer…

I didn't fall on the floor. But I leaned against a cupboard and had no idea how to save the lesson. The disgusted faces of the boys made it worse. It was such a long way from the days when I had been pleading for seriousness and attention.

Then Johnny rose from the floor. He was very white and looked reproachful.

'I feel sick,' he said.

I opened the door and he hurried out.

'And did he get the statue all right?' asked Toll sharply.

I banged an inward eye shut on the crazy vision and spoke hurriedly.

'No,' I said. 'It collapsed.'

Edward Blishen, *Roaring Boys*

1. Find out from examining this passage closely what makes it potentially funny. (Concentrate particularly on its composition, pace, dialogue, and the contrasting attitudes of all those involved.)
2. Recount the funniest incident you can remember in a classroom. (Remember that the humour will be for the reader not only in the nature of the incident itself but in the way you re-tell it.)
3. Humour often lies not in a single incident, however, but in the way a whole string of incidents is put together to make an amusing picture. Here the humour depends heavily on the selection and arrangement of the details and the putting side by side of descriptions and details that leave a small grin of recognition on the reader's face. One such passage comes in Laurie Lee's *Cider with Rosie*. Read it thoughtfully and then compose a quietly humorous description of a classroom in which you sat during your own early days at school:

Our village school was poor and crowded, but in the end I relished it. It had a lively reek of steaming life: boys' boots, girls' hair, stoves and sweat, blue ink, white chalk and shavings. We learnt nothing abstract or tenuous there — just simple patterns of facts and letters, portable tricks of calculation, no more than was needed to measure a shed, write out a bill, read a swine-disease warning. Through the dead hours of the morning, through the long afternoons, we chanted away at our tables. Passers-by could hear our rising voices in our bottled-up room on the bank: 'Twelve-inches-one-foot. Three-feet-make-a-yard. Fourteen-pounds-make-a-stone. Eight-stone-a-hundred-weight.' We absorbed these figures as primal truths declared by some ultimate power. Unhearing, unquestioning, we rocked to our chanting, hammering the gold nails home. 'Twice-two-are-four. One-God-we-love. One-Lord-is-King. One-King-is-George. One-George-is-Fifth...' So it was always; had been; would be for ever; we asked no questions; we didn't hear what we said; yet neither did we ever forget it.

So do I now, through the reiterations of those days, recall that schoolroom which I scarcely noticed — Miss Wardley in glory on her high desk throne, her long throat tinkling with glass. The bubbling stove with its chink of red fire; the old world map as dark as tea; dead field-flowers in jars on the windowsills; the cupboard yawning with dog-eared books. Then the boys and the girls, the dwarfs and the cripples, the slow fat ones and the quick bony ones; giants and louts, angels and squinters — Walt Kerry, Bill Timbrell, Spadge Hopkins, Clergy Green, the Ballingers and Browns, Betty Gleed, Clarry Hogg, Sam and Sixpence, Poppy and Jo — we were ugly and beautiful, scrofulous, warted, ring-wormed and scabbed at the knees; we were noisy, crude, intolerant, cruel, stupid, and superstitious. But we moved together out of the clutch of the Fates, inhabitors of a world without doom; with a scratching, licking, and chewing of pens, a whisper and passing of jokes, a titter of tickling, a grumble of labour, a vague stare at the wall in a dream...

'Oh, miss, please, miss, can I go round the back?'

An unwilling nod permits me. I stamp out noisily into a swoop of fresh air and a musical surge of birds. All round me now is the free green world, with Mrs Birt hanging out her washing.

Laurie Lee, *Cider with Rosie*

Humour in **poetry** seems all too often to be trivial, but lurking behind the seemingly superficial lies a deeper truth. Can you see what the truth is behind these short poems?

(a)   SOLDIER FREDDY

Soldier Freddy
   was never ready,
But! Soldier Neddy,
   unlike Freddy
Was *always* ready
   and steady.

That's why,
   When soldier Neddy
Is-outside-Buckingham-Palace-on-guard-in-the-pouring
   wind-and-rain-
     being-steady-and-ready,
Freddy-
   is home in beddy.

Spike Milligan

(b)   Here lies a poor woman who was always tired,
   She lived in a house where help wasn't hired:
   Her last words on earth were: 'Dear friends, I am going
   To where there's no cooking, or washing, or sewing,
   For everything there is exact to my wishes.
   For where they don't eat there's no washing of dishes.
   I'll be where loud anthems will always be ringing,
   But having no voice I'll be quit of the singing.
   Don't mourn for me now, don't mourn for me never,
   I am going to do nothing for ever and ever.'

Anon.

(c)   WHAT'S THE USE
   Sure, deck your lower limbs in pants;
   Yours are the limbs, my sweeting.
   You look divine as you advance—
   Have you seen yourself retreating?

Ogden Nash

(d)   THE ANATOMY OF HUMOUR
   'What is funny?' you ask my child,
   Crinkling your bright-blue eye.
   'Ah, that is a curious question indeed!'
   Musing, I make reply,

   'Contusions are funny, not open wounds,
   And automobiles that go
   Crash into trees by the highwayside;
   Industrial accidents, no.

'The habit of drink is an hundred per cent,
But drug addiction is nil.
A nervous breakdown will get no laughs;
Insanity surely will.

'Humour, aloof from the cigarette,
Inhabits the droll cigar;
The middle-aged are not very funny;
The young and the old, they are.

'So the funniest thing in the world should be
A grandsire, drunk, insane.
Maimed in a motor accident,
And enduring moderate pain.

'But why do you scream and yell, my child?
Here comes your mother, my honey,
To comfort you and to lecture me
For trying, she'll say, to be funny.'

Morris Bishop

Sometimes in poetry, however, the truth and the humour are more profound.
Some of the satirical poems of the eighteenth century when poets drew attention
to follies and abuses and tried to 'laugh people out of them' and some of the
poetry of protest over the ages use humour effectively to sugar the pill of the
teaching and instruction. Two examples of modern satirical poetry will make
the point clear, perhaps. Can you see what they are protesting about?

(*i*) ENGLAND EXPECTS

Let us pause to consider the English,
Who when they pause to consider themselves they get all
    reticently thrilled and tinglish,
Because every Englishman is convinced of one thing, viz:
That to be an Englishman is to belong to the most exclusive club
    there is:
A club to which benighted bounders of Frenchmen and Germans
    and Italians et cetera cannot even aspire to belong,
Because they don't even speak English, and the Americans are
    worst of all because they speak it wrong.
Englishmen are distinguished by their traditions and ceremonials,
And also by their affection for their colonies and the contempt
    for the colonials.
When foreigners ponder world affairs, why sometimes by doubt
    they are smitten,
But Englishmen know instinctively that what the world needs
    most is whatever is best for Great Britain.
They have a splendid navy and they conscientiously admire it,
And every English schoolboy knows that John Paul Jones was
    only an unfair American pirate.
English people disclaim sparkle and verve,

But speak without reservations of their Anglo-Saxon reserve.
After listening to little groups of English ladies and
    gentlemen at cocktail parties and in hotels and
    Pullmans, of defining Anglo-Saxon reserve I despair,
But I think it consists of assuming that nobody else is there,
And I shudder to think where Anglo-Saxon reserve ends
    when I consider where it begins,
Which in a few high-pitched statements of what one's
    income is and just what foods give one a rash
    and whether one and one's husband or wife sleep
    in a double bed or twins.
All good Englishmen go to Oxford or Cambridge, and they
    all write and publish books before graduation,
And I often wondered how they did it until I realised
    that they have to do it because their genteel accents
    are so developed that they can no longer understand
    each other's spoken words and so the written word is their
    only means of inter-communication.
England is the last home of the aristocracy, and the art of
    protecting the aristocracy from the encroachments of commerce
    has been raised to quite an art.
Because in America a rich butter-and-egg man is only
    a rich butter-and-egg man or at most an honorary
    LL.D of some hungry university, but in England he is
    Sir Benjamin Buttery, Bart.
Anyhow, I think the English people are sweet,
And we might as well get used to them because when they
    slip and fall they always land on their own or
    somebody else's feet.

Ogden Nash

Try to write *either* a poem in reply *or* another poem similarly attacking the Americans.

(*ii*) The following poem is a parody of a famous hymn "We plough the fields and scatter The good seed on the land'; it was written by the former poet-laureate John Betjeman who died in 1984:

HARVEST HYMN

We spray the fields and scatter
    The poison on the ground
So that no wicked wild flowers
    Upon our farm be found.
We like whatever helps us
    To line our purse with pence
The twenty-four-hour broiler-house
    And neat electric fence.

All concrete sheds around us
And Jaguars in the yard,
The telly lounge and deep freeze
Are ours from working hard.

We fire the fields for harvest,
   The hedges swell the flame,
The oak trees and the cottages
   From which our fathers came.
We give no compensation,
   The earth is ours today,
And if we lose our arable
   Then bungalows will pay

All concrete sheds ... etc.

John Betjeman

Try to write a parody of a well-known poem by taking as your theme some topic about which you feel strongly and wish to persuade your readers to accept.

Humour in **drama** is complex. On the one hand there are farces which deliberately set out, often grotesquely, to exaggerate actions and characters for comic effect. On the other hand there are moments of comedy, sometimes inserted into deep tragedies (e.g. *King Lear*, *Hamlet* and *Macbeth*), which are poignant. No one action or situation or character in itself is necessarily comic rather than tragic. Someone slipping on a banana skin is not funny if someone breaks his or her back in doing so; there is nothing funny necessarily about infidelity in marriage or insanity or deformity; a man at whom the world laughs is not necessarily at all a comic character.

There are numerous theories about humour in drama. For example, we laugh at those things which make us inwardly afraid or we laugh at the grotesque or things which seem not to fit somehow or we laugh at things that surprise us or are out of context, etc. Comedy is not easy to write, direct, or play as those in the theatre will quickly tell you.

However, read the following extracts from plays and in your English group discuss where the real humour in the scene lies. Then write up an account of your findings for your English file. You may even like, after some improvisation work, to create a comic scene in your drama work.

(*a*) Arnold Wesker's play *Chips with Everything* concerns the training of a group of young men conscripted into the RAF. It was presented by the English Stage Company at the Royal Court Theatre on 27 April 1962 with Frank Finlay in one of the major parts:

Sound of marching feet. Marching stops. The lecture hall. Boys enter and sit on seats. Enter WING COMMANDER; boys rise.

Wing Commander:	Sit down, please. I'm your Wing Commander. You think we are at peace. Not true. We are never at peace. The human being is in a constant state of war and we must be prepared, each against the other. History has taught us this and we must learn. The reasons why and wherefore are not our concern. We are simply the men who must be prepared. You, why do you look at me like that?
Pip:	I'm paying attention, sir.
Wing Commander:	There's insolence in those eyes, lad — I recognise insolence in a man; take that glint out of your eyes, your posh tones don't fool me. We are simply the men who must be prepared. Already the aggressors have a force far superior to ours. Our efforts must be intensified. We need a fighting force, and it is for this reason you are being trained here, according to the best traditions of the R.A.F. We want you to be proud of your past, unashamed of the uniform you wear. But you must not grumble too much if you find that government facilities for you, personally, are not up to standard. We haven't the money to spare… Why are you smiling?
Smiler:	I'm not, sir. It's natural. I was born like it.
Wing Commander:	Because I want this taken seriously, you know, from all of you. Any questions?
Wilfe:	Sir, if the aggressors are better off than us, what are they waiting for?
Wing Commander:	What's your name?
Wilfe:	247 Seaford, sir.
Wing Commander:	Any other questions?
	(*Exits*)
	(*After being addressed by a Squadron Leader and a Pilot Officer the boys are confronted by an NCO, the PT Instructor.*)
NCO:	As you were, I'm in charge of physical training on this camp. It's my duty to see that every minute muscle in your body is awake. Awake and ringing. Do you hear that? That's poetry! I want your body awake and ringing. I want you so light on your feet that the smoke from a cigarette could blow you away, and yet so strong that you stand firm before hurricanes. I hate thin men and detest fat ones. I want you like Greek Gods. You heard of the Greeks? You ignorant troupe of anaemics, you were brought up on tinned beans and television sets, weren't you? You haven't had any exercise since you played knock-down-ginger, have you? Greek Gods, you hear me? Till the sweat pours out of you like Niagara Falls. Did you hear that poetry? Sweat like Niagara Falls! I don't want your stupid questions!
	(*Exits*)

(*b*) The following scene is from Shakespeare's *A Midsummer Night's Dream*. A group of workmen have decided to put on a play, *Pyramus* and Thisby in front of the Duke and Duchess of Venice. Peter Quince, a carpenter, is the self-appointed director of the play. Bottom a weaver, sees himself as the star and wants to play all the parts.

Examine the scene carefully to see where the humour lies. Think particularly about the members of the cast, the parts they want, and the way the language is terribly abused by them. Then write up your views about the humour in the scene for your English course-work file.

Try, with the help of your English or Drama group, to play out the scene. Some 'ham' acting could well be in order, perhaps?

Quince: Is all our company here?

Bottom: You were best to call them generally, man by man, according to the scrip.

Quince: Here is the scroll of every man's name, which is thought fit, through all Athens, to play in our interlude before the duke and duchess on his wedding at night.

Bottom: First, good Peter Quince, say what the play treats on; then read the names of the actors, and so grow to a point.

Quince: Marry, our play is, The most lamentable comedy, and most cruel death of Pyramus and Thisby.

Bottom: A very good piece of work, I assure you, and a merry. Now, good Peter Quince, call forth your actors by the scroll. Masters, spread yourselves.

Quince: Answer as I call you. Nick Bottom, the weaver.

Bottom: Ready. Name what part I am for, and proceed.

Quince: You, Nick Bottom, are set down for Pyramus.

Bottom: What is Pyramus? a lover, or a tyrant?

Quince: A lover, that kills himself most gallantly for love.

Bottom: That will ask some tears in the true performing of it: if I do it, let the audience look to their eyes; I will move storms, I will condole in some measure. To the rest: yet my chief humour is for a tyrant. I could play Ercles rarely, or a part to tear a cat in, to make all split... Now name the rest of the players.

Quince: Francis Flute, the bellows-mender.

Flute: Here, Peter Quince.

Quince: You must take Thisby on you.

Flute: What is Thisby? a wandering knight?

Quince: It is the lady that Pyramus must love.

Flute: Nay, faith, let me not play a woman; I have a beard coming.

Quince: That's all one: you shall play it in a mask, and you may speak as small as you will.

Bottom: An I may hide my face, let me play Thisby too. I'll speak in a monstrous little voice, 'Thisne, Thisne!? 'Ah Pyramus, my lover dear; thy Thisby dear, and lady dear!'

Quince: No, no, you must play Pyramus; and Flute, you Thisby.

Bottom: Well, proceed.

Quince: Robin Starveling, the tailor.

Starveling: Here, Peter Quince.

Quince: Robin Starveling, you must play Thisby's mother. Tom Snout, the tinker.

Snout: Here, Peter Quince.

Quince: You, Pyramus's father; myself, Thisby's father; Snug, the joiner, you the lion's part: and, I hope, here is a play fitted.

Snug: Have you the lion's part written? pray you, if it be, give it me, for I am slow of study.

Quince: You may do it extempore*, for it is nothing but roaring.

Bottom: Let me play the lion, too. I will roar, that I will do any man's heart good to hear me; I will roar, that I will make the duke say, 'Let him roar again, let him roar again.'

Quince: An you should do it too terribly, you would fright the duchess and the ladies that they would shriek; and that were enough to hang us all.

All: That would hang us, every mother's son.

Bottom: I grant you, friends, if that you should fright the ladies out of their wits, they would have no more discretion but to hang us; but I will aggravate my voice so that I will roar you as gently as any sucking dove; I will roar you as 'twere any nightingale.

Quince: You can play no part by Pyramus; for Pyramus is a sweet-faced man; a proper man, as one shall see in a summer's day; a most lovely gentleman-like man; therefore you must needs play Pyramus.

Bottom: Well, I will undertake it. What beard were I best to play it in?

Quince: Why, what you will...But masters, here are your parts; and I am to entreat you, request you, and desire you, to con them by tomorrow night, and meet me in the palace wood, a mile without the town, by moonlight: there will we rehearse; for if we meet in the city, we shall be dogged with company, and our devices known. In the meantime I will draw a bill of properties, such as our play wants. I pray you, fail me not.

Bottom: We will meet; and there we may rehearse more obscenely and courageously. Take pains; be perfect; adieu.

Quince: At the duke's oak we meet.

(Act 1, scene 2)

Find another comic scene from Shakespeare's plays. How does the humour in it differ from that here? (Begin by looking at *Henry IV, Part One*, with Falstaff, *Much Ado about Nothing* with Dogberry, and *Hamlet* with the gravediggers, perhaps.)

 Humour is not limited to texts in literature. Cartoons, photographs and paintings, and music can also be full of humour.

(a) *Punch*, of course, is probably the best known magazine which makes use of cartoons to make its point. On pages 93 and 94 are two such drawings, one laughing at a contemporary craze for marathons — seeing how long people could keep going at one activity, and the other poking mild fun at pop festivals.

* Off-the-cuff, as it comes.

Choose a subject of your own and draw a picture, with or without a caption, which will make others laugh, and makes a point.

(b) Write a story based on a photograph you have at home and which you find quite amusing or which reminds you of an amusing time you once had. Include the photo with your work. Your English group might like to assemble a collection of humorous photographs they have discovered — or, indeed, taken themselves. Some family snapshot albums contain one or two unexpected surprises! Why not mount an exhibition?

(*c*) The comic operas of Gilbert and Sullivan, written between 1875 and 1896 contain much more social satire and are full of humorous characters and comic situations. Some songs and ballads, too, carry comic twists to them — often in the last few lines. But music without words can sometimes be humorous, where the composer surprises his listeners by unusual effects such as the clog dance in the ballet *La fille mal gardée* (a kind of pantomime, almost) or Mozart's use of sleigh bells set alongside the pomp of the opening bars in his German dance (K.605 No. 3) or Elgar's making fun of one of his friends' difficulties in sight-reading in *Enigma Variations* (Opus 36). Can you think of other examples of humour in music?

 Finally, here is a piece of writing based on a popular TV series, *Porridge*, in which Ronnie Barker starred. Notice particularly how the language, characters, and situation blend together to form a deeply comic situation:

The high spot of your convict's life is, in most cases, visiting time. I have known instances in which the arrival of the loved one is not an unmixed delight. In fact, I recall a bloke I shared a cell with once in Brixton for whom the chance to commune with his nearest and dearest was pure hell. He was a very hard man inside and had everyone, including some of the screws, in a state of abject terror. But when his old woman faced him across the table he dwindled into a cross between a worm and a jelly. Still, I had no problems along those lines, having an excellent relationship with my wife and a strong paternal affection for my kids. It was thus with keen delight that I saw my eldest girl, Ingrid, swaying down the central aisle towards me.

'Hello, dad,' she called cheerily.

'Hello, Ingrid, love.'

Ingrid seated herself opposite me and gave me a big, warm smile. Someone tapped me on the shoulder and, turning, I found Lennie smiling in a deferential way. He was seated at the next table, opposite a grey-haired old bint. Either that's not Denise, I thought to myself, or young Godber needs straightening out. However, he immediately reassured me by saying, 'Oh-er-this is me mum, Fletch.'

At this, the old mother-of-pearl leaned towards me and smiled primly. I didn't waste time on other people's visitors but courtesy demanded some response. So I stood up and said, 'Great pleasure, Mrs Godber. Got a fine lad there. This is my eldest, Ingrid.'

Ingrid also offered a smile but I noticed that it seemed to be aimed more towards Lennie than his mum. Just then a roar like a nearby building collapsing caused us to jump. It turned out to be MacKay registering disapproval at our little social gathering which was against regulations.

'Sit down, Fletcher. And you, Godber. This is not a royal garden party.'

'Who's he, then?' asked Ingrid, when the reverberations had subsided.

'That's Mr MacKay. Charmless Celtic nark.'

'And who's the boy?'

'Oh, that's Lennie. Lennie Godber, my temporary cell-mate. He's from Birmingham but he's got an O-level in Geography. Need to, I should think, to find your way round Birmingham. Well what's the news? How's your mother then?'

'Oh fine, dad. Sends her love and everything.'

A few days later Godber signed a letter and then wrote out the envelope. He handed it to me.

'Fletch, could you get your mucker Barrowclough to post if for me?'

I inspected the envelope. It was addressed to the BBC. 'Oh no,' I exclaimed. 'You're not still trying to meet that slag Denise, are you?'

But he shook his head happily. 'No, not her.'

'Well, who?'

'Ingrid.'

'Oh, Ing — WHO?'

'That's right, Fletch, your daughter. Our eyes met and I knew — I knew — you don't mind, Fletch, do you?'

I shook my head to clear the black mist.

'Mind?' I asked faintly and then more vigorously. 'MIND? You think I'd let my beloved Ingrid take up with the likes of you? A bleeding juvenile delinquent from the back streets of Birmingham? A con, a thief, a-a-a'

'A chip off the old block,' suggested Lennie cheerfully. 'Now, how about a game of ping-pong, dad?'

Dick Clement and Ian le Frenais, *Another Stretch of Porridge*

Write a scene where the situation, the conversation, and the characters are clearly linked to provide comedy. Bear in mind that the scene is intended for TV showing and must have a wide appeal. *Alternatively*, write up a scene from a comedy series you have seen recently, retaining some of the dialogue but adding your own comments to explain how the words were said and what the actions were, similar to those in the scene from *Porridge*.

Unit 7

Truth is stranger than fiction

'Tis strange — but true; for truth is always strange;
Stranger than fiction.

Lord Byron

This unit explores some strange events that seem to baffle explanation. Some of them are true and some of them are fictional but all of them surprise and even astound. No doubt, you have had some uncanny experiences yourself which you can bring to your work here and speak and write about.

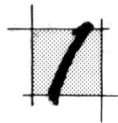

First, consider the following strange events — all of which actually happened:

(*a*) Dora Watkinson trod on a darning needle one day, and part of it broke off and entered her foot. the foot was X-rayed, and a fragment of the needle removed. She appeared to feel no ill-effects. About a year later, however, her tongue started to scratch on something in her jaw— and she removed from between two of her lower teeth half an inch of the broken needle trodden on twelve months earlier. It had toured her body through the bloodstream.

(*b*) In 1982 a child was born in the United States with a bullet in his brain. His 17-year-old mother gave birth to the boy more than two months premature after she was shot in a love-triangle quarrel. The bullet passed through her lower back and through her kidney before lodging in the brain of the unborn child. The boy, Daniel, was delivered by Caesarian section several hours later. He was put on a life-support system and it was two months before the operating team at Broward General Hospital in Florida felt able to remove the bullet. The *Daily Mirror*, which carried the story stated that Daniel was now growing up into a perfectly normal toddler.

(*c*) Tricia Reay, aged 12, appropriately enough from Sutton Coldfield, scored a world record for Britain by sneezing non-stop for 156 days; and still she kept on sneezing, on average, once every twenty seconds. Relief was to come eventually when she was taken from her home to a clinic in the Pyrenees where doctors managed to cure her condition. From October 1979, when she caught a cold, to 29 April 1980, Tricia had sneezed for over 200 days.

(*d*) In 1977 a four-legged boy was born in a Lincolnshire hospital, and moved to Sheffield Children's Hospital. After six weeks, doctors prepared to carry out the rare and delicate operation of removing the handicap. According to a newspaper report of 22 March in that year, the operation was a success and the child doing well.

1. Hunt through old copies of newspapers and magazines in your reference library to see if you can add three or more examples of strange happenings to these four. Then write one of them up fully.
2. One book on such topics (*Strange But True*, edited by Tim Healey in 1983) from which these extracts were taken, also gives incidents of where black people turned white and white people turned black. What differences would such a change make to your life if it were to happen to you?

Drama and other fiction also recount strange events from time to time. Bottom's transformation through magic in Shakespeare's *A Midsummer Night's Dream* results in his having his head replaced with that of an ass. The hero of H. G. Wells's short story, *The Truth about Pyecroft*, finds the secret of how to lose weight and float up to the ceiling to the concern of his friends.

1. Give an account, either in writing for your English file, or orally to your English group of the strangest two or three events you have come across in books of fiction.

It is in ghost stories, however, that some of the oddest things happen.

At that moment the door opened, and Mr Carter came in, rubbing his hands. He was a dentist, and washed them before and after everything he did. 'You!' said his wife. 'Home already!'

'Not unwelcome, I hope,' said Mr Carter nodding to Betty. 'Two people cancelled their appointments: I decided to come home. I said, I hope I am not unwelcome.'

'Silly!' said his wife. 'Of course not.'

'Small Simon seems doubtful,' continued Mr Carter. 'Small Simon, are you sorry to see me at tea with you?'

'No, Daddy':

'No, what?'

'No, Big Simon.'

'That's right. Big Simon and Small Simon. That sounds more like friends, doesn't it? At one time little boys had to call their father "sir". If they forgot— a good spanking. On the bottom, Small Simon, on the bottom!' said Mr Carter, washing his hands once more with his invisible soap and water.

The little boy turned crimson with shame or rage.

'But now, you see,' said Betty, to help, 'you can call your father whatever you like.'

'And what', asked Mr Carter, 'has Small Simon been doing this afternoon? While Big Simon has been at work?'

'Nothing,' muttered his son.

'Then you have been bored,' said Mr Carter. 'Learn from experience, Small Simon. Tomorrow, do something amusing, and you will not be bored. I want him to learn from experience, Betty. That is my way, the new way.'

'I have learned,' said the boy, speaking like an old, tired man, as little boys so often do.

'It would hardly seem so,' said Mr Carter, 'if you sit on your behind all the afternoon doing nothing. Had *my* father caught me doing nothing I should not have sat very comfortably.'

'He played,' said Mrs Carter.

'A bit,' said the boy, shifting on his chair.

'Too much,' said Mrs Carter. 'He comes in all nervy and dazed. He ought to have his rest.'

'He is six,' said her husband. 'He is a reasonable being. He must choose for himself. But what game is this, Small Simon, that is worth getting nervy and dazed over? There are very few games as good as all that.'

'It's nothing.' said the boy.

'Oh, come,' said his father. 'We are friends, are we not? You can tell me. I was a Small Simon once, just like you, and played the same games you play. Of course there were no aeroplanes in those days. With whom do you play this fine game? Come on, we must all answer civil questions, or the world would never go round. With whom do you play?'

'Mr Beelzy,' said the boy, unable to resist.

'Mr Beelzy?' said his father, raising his eyebrows inquiringly at his wife.

'It's a game he makes up,' she said.

'Not makes up!' cried the boy. 'Fool!'

'That is telling stories,' said his mother. 'And rude as well. We had better talk of something different.'

'No wonder he is rude,' said Mr Carter, 'if you say he tells lies, and then insist on changing the subject. He tells you his fantasy: you implant a guilt feeling. What can you expect? A defence mechanism. Then you get a real lie.'

'Like in *These Three*,' said Betty, 'only different, of course. *She* was an unblushing little liar.'

'I would have made her blush,' said Mr Carter, 'in the proper part of her anatomy. But Small Simon is in the fantasy stage. Are you not, Small Simon? You just make things up.'

'No, I don't', said the boy.

'You do,' said his father. 'And because you do, it is not too late to reason with you. There is no harm in a fantasy, old chap. There is no harm in a bit of make-believe. Only you have to know the difference between day-dreams and real things, or your brain will never grow. It will never be the brain of a Big Simon. So come on. Let us hear about this Mr Beelzy of yours. Come on. What is he like?'

'He isn't like anything,' said the boy.

'Like nothing on earth?' said his father. 'That's a terrible fellow.'

'I'm not frightened of him,' said the child, smiling. 'Not a bit.'

'I should hope not,' said his father. 'If you were, you would be frightening yourself. I am always telling people, older people than you are, that they are just frightening themselves. Is he a funny man? Is he a giant?'

'Sometimes he is,' said the little boy.

'Sometimes one thing, sometimes another,' said his father. 'Sounds pretty vague. Why can't you tell us just what he's like?'

'I love him,' said the small boy. 'He loves me.'

'That's a big word,' said Mr Carter. 'That might be better kept for real things like Big Simon and Small Simon.'

'He *is* real,' said the boy, passionately. 'He's not a fool. He's real.'

'Listen,' said his father. 'When you go down the garden there's nobody there, is there?'

'No,' said the boy.

'Then you think of him, inside your head, and he comes.'

'No,' said Small Simon. 'I have to do something with my stick.'

'That doesn't matter.'

'Yes, it does.'

'Small Simon, you are being obstinate.' said Mr Carter. 'I am trying to explain something to you. I have been longer in the world than you have, so naturally I am older and wiser. I am explaining that Mr Beelzy is a fantasy of yours. Do you hear? Do you understand?'

'Yes, Daddy.'

'He is a game. He is a let's-pretend.'

The little boy looked down at his plate, smiling resignedly.

'I hope you are listening to me,' said his father. 'All you have to do is to say, "I have been playing a game of let's-pretend. With someone I make up, called Mr Beelzy". Then no-one will say you tell lies, and you will know the difference between dreams and reality. Mr Beelzy is a day-dream.'

The little boy still stared at his plate.

'He is sometimes there and sometimes not there,' pursued Mr Carter. 'Sometimes he's like one thing, sometimes another. You can't really see him. Not as you see me. I am real. You can't touch him. You can touch me. I can touch you.' Mr Carter stretched out his big, white, dentist's hand, and took his little son by the shoulder. He stopped speaking for a moment and tightened his hand. The little boy sank his head still lower.

'Now you know the difference,' said Mr Carter, 'between a pretend and a real thing. You and I are one thing, he is another. Which is the pretend? Come on. Answer me. Which is the pretend?'

'Big Simon and Small Simon,' said the little boy.

'Don't!' cried Betty, and at once put her hand over her mouth, for why should a visitor cry 'Don't' when a father is explaining things in a scientific and modern way?

'Well, my boy,' said Mr Carter, 'I have said you must be allowed to learn from experience. Go upstairs. Right up to your room. You shall learn whether it is better to reason, or to be perverse and obstinate. Go up. I shall follow you.'

'You are not going to beat the child?' cried Mrs Carter.

'No.' said the little boy. 'Mr Beelzy won't let him.'

Small Simon stopped at the door. 'He said he wouldn't let anyone hurt me,' he whimpered. 'He said he'd come like a lion, with wings on, and eat them up.'

'You'll learn how real he is!' shouted his father after him. 'If you can't learn it at one end, you shall learn it at the other. I'll have your breeches down. I shall finish my cup of tea first, however,' he said to the two women.

Neither of them spoke. Mr Carter finished his tea, and unhurriedly left the room, washing his hands with his invisible soap and water.

Mrs Carter said nothing. Betty could think of nothing to say. She wanted to be talking: she was afraid of what they might hear.

Suddenly it came. It seemed to tear the air apart. 'Good God!' she cried. 'What was that? He's hurt him.' She sprang out of her chair, her silly eyes flashing behind her glasses. 'I'm going up there!' she cried, trembling.

'Yes, let us go up,' said Mrs Carter. 'Let us go up. That was not Small Simon.'

It was on the second-floor landing that they found the shoe, with the man's foot still in it, like that last morsel of a mouse which sometimes falls from the jaws of a hasty cat.

John Collier, *Thus I Refute Beelzy* (abridged)

2. Do you believe in ghosts? What is your view based on? Discuss with your English group some of the following topics:
   (a) evidence of the paranormal;
   (b) life after death and life before birth;
   (c) poltergeists; seances;
   (d) ghost stories you have read.

3. Then try to write a ghost story of your own. Remember that the best ghost stories (e.g. Henry James's *The Turning of the Screw*) succeed quite often

because they insist on placing the supernatural in the context of what is normal — even mundane, just as John Collier's story was placed amidst an ordinary and somewhat trivial family quarrel.

4. Some other ghostly or strange events you might like to read about and investigate are: the mystery of the *Marie Celeste* (a ghost ship found sailing in the middle of the Atlantic without crew or passengers a hundred years ago); ghosts in the Bloody Tower of the Tower of London; ghosts of the theatre — especially at Drury Lane; the ghostly happenings in Coleridge's poem *The Ancient Mariner*.

 Now for some strange events in poetry, some just as strange and bizarre as the ship with its crew made up of the dead in *The Ancient Mariner*.

(*a*) First, a poem about a nightmare written by Wilfred Owen, a British officer killed on the Sambre Canal in France a week before the Great War of 1914–18 ended:

STRANGE MEETING

It seemed that out of battle I escaped
Down some profound dull tunnel, long since scooped
Through granites which titanic wars had groined.
Yet also there encumbered sleepers groaned,
Too fast in thought or death to be bestirred.
Then, as I probed them, one sprang up, and stared
With piteous recognition in fixed eyes,
Lifting distressful hands as if to bless
And by his smile I knew that sullen hall,
By his dead smile I knew we stood in Hell.
With a thousand pains that vision's face was grained;
Yet no blood reached there from the upper ground,
And no guns thumped, or down the flues made moan.
'Strange friend,' I said, 'here is no cause to mourn.'
'None,' said the other, 'save the undone years,
The hopelessness. Whatever hope is yours,
Was my life also; I went hunting wild
After the wildest beauty in the world,
Which lies not calm in eyes, nor braided hair,
But mocks the steady running of the hour,
And if it grieves, grieves richlier than here.
For by my glee might many men have laughed,
And of my weeping something had been left,
Which must die now. I mean the truth untold,
The pity of war, the pity war distilled.
Now men will go content with what we spoiled.
Or, discontent, boil bloody, and be spilled.
They will be swift with swiftness of the tigress,
None will break ranks, though nations trek from progress.

Courage was mine and I had mystery,
Wisdom was mine, and I had mastery.
To miss the march of this retreating world
Into vain citadels that are not walled.
Then, when much blood had clogged their chariot-wheels
I would go up and wash them from sweet wells.
Even with truths that lie too deep for taint.
I would have poured my spirit without stint
But not through wounds; not on the cess of war.
Foreheads of men have bled where no wounds were.
I am the enemy you killed, my friend.
I knew you in this dark; for so you frowned
Yesterday through me as you jabbed and killed.
I parried; but my hands were loath and cold.
Let us sleep now…

Wilfred Owen

This poem needs to be read aloud and listened to. What do you notice about its sound? What has happened to the rhyme? Why is this?

The poem is in the form of a dialogue between two soldiers. Write your own dialogue of two characters in a dream or a nightmare you have had. (It need not be in verse, if you would rather write in prose.)

(*b*) The second poem is also about a nightmare, but it is in quite a different mood. It is written by W. S. Gilbert, the man who wrote the lyrics for the comic operas referred to in Unit Six:

NIGHTMARE

When you're lying awake with a dismal headache, and repose is
taboo'd by anxiety,
I conceive you may use any language you choose to indulge in,
without impropriety;
For your brain is on fire—the bedclothes conspire of usual
slumber to plunder you:
First your counterpane goes, and uncovers your toes, and your
sheet slips demurely from you;
Then the blanketing tickles—you feel like mixed pickles—so
terribly sharp is the pricking,
And you're hot, and you're cross, and you tumble and toss
till there's nothing 'twixt you and the ticking.
Then the bedclothes all creep to the ground in a heap, and you
pick 'em all up in a tangle;
Next your pillow resigns and politely declines to remain at its
usual angle;
Well, you get some repose in the form of a doze, with hot
eye-balls and head ever aching.
But your slumbering teems with such horrible dreams that
you'd very much better be waking;
For you dream you are crossing the Channel, and tossing about
in a steamer from Harwich—

Which is something between a large bathing machine and a very
small second-class carriage—
And you're giving a treat (penny ice and cold meat) to a party
of friends and relations—
They're a ravenous horde—and they all came on board at
Sloane Square and South Kensington Stations.
And bound on that journey you find your attorney (who started
that morning from Devon);
He's a bit undersized, and you don't feel surprised when he
tells you he's only eleven.
Well, you're driving like mad with a singular lad (by-the-by the
ship's now a four-wheeler).
And you're playing round games, and he calls you bad names
when you tell him that 'ties pay the dealer';
But this you can't stand, so you throw up your hand, and you
find you're as cold as an icicle,
In your shirt and your socks (the black silk with gold clocks),
crossing Salisbury Plain on a bicycle:
And he and the crew are on bicycles too—which they've
somehow or other invested in—
And he's telling the tars, all the particulars of a company
he's interested in—
It's a scheme of devices, to get at low prices, all goods
from cough mixtures to cables
(Which tickled the sailors) by treating retailers, as though
they were all vegetables—
You get a good spadesman to plant a small tradesman
(first take off his boots with a boot-tree),
And his legs will take root, and his fingers will shoot,
and they'll blossom and bud like a fruit-tree—
From the greengrocer tree you get grapes and green pea,
cauliflower, pineapple, and cranberries,
While the pastrycook plant, cherry brandy will grant,
apple puffs, and three-corners, and banberries—
The shares are a penny, and ever so many are taken by
ROTHSCHILD and BARING,
And just as a few are allotted to you, you awake with a
shudder despairing—
You're a regular wreck, with a crick in your neck, and
no wonder you snore, for your head's on the floor, and
you've needles and pins from your soles to your
shins, and your flesh is a-creep for your left
leg's asleep, and you've cramp in your toes, and
a fly on your nose, and some fluff in your
lung, and a feverish tongue, and a thirst
that's intense, and a general sense that you haven't
been sleeping in clover;
But the darkness has passed, and it's daylight at last,
and the night has been long—ditto ditto my song—
and thank goodness both of them are over!

W. S. Gilbert

One of the features of a nightmare which Gilbert uses in his poem is the way one incident links with and runs on to the next. Nevertheless, in the middle of all the connections there is a fundamental lack of continuity resulting in a mixed-up jumble of details. Try to describe your own nightmare (one which may come back again and again, incidentally) as part of an English group's discussion on dreams. Then try to write it up as graphically as you can — in verse, if you wish.

(c) Thirdly, here are a series of short poems of an unusual and bizarre kind; they are all about the dear departed!

(i) Beneath this slab
John Brown is stowed.
He watched the ads
And not the road.

Ogden Nash

(ii) Here lies the body of Mary Ann Lowder,
She burst while drinking a seidlitz powder.
Called from this world to her heavenly rest,
She should have waited till it effervesced.

Anon.

(iii) Billy, in one of his nice new sashes,
Fell in the fire and was burnt to ashes;
Now, although the room goes chilly,
I haven't the hart to poke poor Billy.

Harry Graham

(iv) Mary Ann has gone to rest,
Safe at last on Abraham's breast,
Which may be nuts for Mary Anne,
But is certainly rough on Abraham.

Anon.

(v) When Bibo thought fit from the world to retreat,
As full of Champagne as an egg's full of meat,
He wak'd in the boat; and to CHARON* he said,
He wou'd be row'd back, for he was not yet dead.
Trim the boat, and sit quiet, stern CHARON reply'd:
You may have forgot, you were drunk when you dy'd.

Matthew Prior

Write two or three epitaphs in similar vein – trying to draw attention to the strange and bizarre.

* *Charon* is the boatsman who, in Greek legend, ferried the dead to the next world.

Newspapers are always on the look-out for the unusual. Here are a few reports:

(*a*) Mrs Poppy Hull, an accountant, was strolling to work down Chertsey Road in Woking, Surrey. She felt what she thought was a pair of arms on her shoulders. Mrs Hull turned and saw that it was a lion. She collapsed. The lion stood over her until its owner arrived at the scene.

The lion's name was Shane and he was the 14-stone plaything of Mr Ronald Voice who kept his pet in an old double-decker bus. Mr Voice had been playing with the lion in his back garden. It was not clear why it had approached Mrs Hull, unless it was because she was wearing a leopard-skin coat.

(*b*) Police are scouring the slopes of one of China's holiest mountains for three mugger monkeys who have been robbing tourists and pilgrims. Each of the three old monkeys has a physical defect. One is hare-lipped, another is one-eyed, and the third has only three fingers on its right hand. The terrible trio has been attacking visitors to Omei mountain in the central district of China and stealing watches and bags. Tourists are advised to bring food as a bribe to distract the monkeys' attention, making escape possible.

(*c*) *Johannesburg, Tuesday*. A motorist shot a hare and threw it into the back seat of his car.
The hare was only stunned and, regaining consciousness, touched off the trigger of the gun as it leapt out of the window.
The shot wounded the motorist in the neck.

1. Imagine that you are interviewing one of the people involved in one of the incidents given above or in one of the strange tales you have found yourself in newspapers. Write out the dialogue that followed between you.
2. Invent some bizarre stories of your own that might have been found in newspapers and mingle them with others that are real reports. Ask other members of your English group to say which are the 'invented' and which are the 'real' reports and to give their reasons for their views.

The following section is on strange people.

(*a*) The first passage describes George 'Beau' Brummell (1778–1840):

He made the cravat his trademark. It took him three hours to tie and was a snowy froth of fine starched muslin. One speck of dust, one crease, and a cravat was tossed aside and the whole ritual of tying it would begin again. The floor of his dressing room was often littered ankle-deep with yards of discarded muslin. 'These are our failures,' explained his valet.

Brummell lived for the art of dressing. His style influenced an age and made him a legend. He would not leave his room until the figure he saw reflected in the mirror was groomed to ultimate perfection.

Three people were involved in making his gloves, one specialising in the thumb alone. His valet polished the soles of his boots as well as the uppers. Once, when a friend asked him what blacking he used to give his boots such magnificent shine, Brummell exclaimed: 'Blacking! I never use blacking. I use nothing but the froth of champagne.'

He was not particularly handsome. He had reddish fair hair, thick lips which he liked to pout, and cool eyes. But his figure was perfectly proportioned and his elegance unsurpassed. It took him two hours to wash. After shaving he would pluck out any offending hair with a pair of silver tweezers. Before dressing he scrubbed his whole body with a stiff brush until he was as 'red as a lobster'. He changed his shirt three times a day and sent his linen to be laundered in the country so that it would smell of new-mown hay. His laundry bills were astronomical.

M. Nicholas, *The World's Greatest Cranks and Crankpots*

Accounts such as this are in the long line of traditional descriptions of people that go back at least as far as Geoffrey Chaucer (1340–1400) who described individually each one of his pilgrims before they set off on a pilgrimage to Canterbury (*The Canterbury Tales*). His description of the Prioress's meticulous style of dressing and her mannerisms are not dissimilar perhaps to Beau Brummell's.

Describe the appearance of someone you know well, preferably somebody who takes enormous care with his or her clothes and appearance.

(*b*)The second passage describes another eccentric from the same period as Beau Brummell, John Cleves Symmes (1780–1892), an American from New Jersey, obsessed with the idea of hollowness.

After studying the universe, John Cleves Symmes, came to the conclusion that the Earth must be hollow, with room inside for five other planets. He was quite positive, moreover, that there were gaping holes at both the North and South Poles and that it was possible to sail into them to find out what was going on inside. He confidently expected to discover another race of human beings, swarming animal life and luxurious vegetation: perhaps even the answer to the mystery of life itself. So convincing was Symmes, and so persuasive a talker, that in January 1823 United States congressmen were prepared to listen politely to a request to finance his proposed expedition to the centre of the earth. (Jules Verne's book *Voyage to the Centre of the Earth* did not come until 1864!)

Symmes drew up his plans with meticulous detail. He had decided, he explained, to tackle the North Pole first. For this attempt he would need 100 'brave companions', including scientists, two ships, and enough reindeer and sleighs to carry his expedition over the frozen wastes of Siberia, from where he planned to set out. He would sail to the hole — which he estimated was 4000 feet in diameter — through the Baring Strait. Asked whether he expected to drop off the edge, he solemnly replied that he rather thought they would just sail on and eventually find themselves inside. They might not even know the historic moment at which they entered the bowels of the earth!

The idea of a hollow planet seemed more and more logical to him. After all, hadn't nature made the interior of animal bones, wheat stalks and human hair completely hollow? Sitting looking at the Universe through his telescope he came to the conclusion that Sir Isaac Newton had been barking up the wrong tree and that an atmosphere 'filled with microscopically invisible hollow spheres of ether' accounted for gravity.

M. Nicholas, *The World's Greatest Cranks and Crackpots*

There have been many strange theories and many strange scientists. *See what you can find out about alchemy or those who began the Flat-Earth Society.* Equally, other scientists who discovered the truth sometimes had a hard time to prove their theories to others and were persecuted for their ideas: e.g. Copernicus; Galileo; and William Harvey, who discovered the circulation of the blood and so opened up the field to modern medicine and surgery. *See what you can find out about a great scientist whose views and theories were not accepted at first.*

1. Give an account of what you discover on the track of the 'mad' scientists.
2. Invent a wild theory of your own and then try to defend it in discussion in your English group *and/or* set it out as persuasively as you can.

(*c*) The third passage describes Frances Henry Egerton, the eighth Earl of Bridgwater, who lived about the same time as Brummell and Symmes and died in 1829; his behaviour was eccentric, to say the least:

Nothing was good enough for his dogs. That to everyone's astonishment, included providing them with the finest and softest leather boots for all four feet. These boots cost him as much as his own, but the man who made them was only too happy to oblige. Egerton had a passion for footwear which he could well afford to indulge. He himself wore a new pair of boots every day of the year. The hundreds of pairs he had discarded were arranged in orderly rows around the walls of his house and used as a calendar to count the days of the year.

A lonely man, who seldom invited anyone to visit him or to dine, he seemed to prefer canine company. He often took half a dozen or more dogs riding with him in his carriage and every day he dined with his four-footed friends. He would have the table set for twelve places and then his favourite dogs were brought in with napkins tied round their necks. Dressed in the height of fashion for these extraordinary meals, with servants behind their chairs to attend to every want, they were expected to eat from plates while he conversed with them. The Earl said his dogs behaved themselves as well as any gentlemen — 'with decent decorum'. If one of them happened to behave literally like a dog, it was banished from the table until it had learned better manners.

M. Nicholas, *The World's Greatest Cranks and Crankpots*

Do you know anyone whose behaviour towards their pets is eccentric? Give an account of what he or she does.

Do you know of anyone who is wildly eccentric in some other way? History books and newspapers are often full of such strange people — give a description of such an eccentric who has interested you recently.

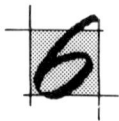 This final section deals with some examples of fantasy in literature, where the writer's imagination takes the reader deliberately into a world where the characters and the setting are not realistic and yet which make their own comments about the world we live in.

(*a*) *Alice's Adventures in Wonderland*, published in 1865, is often thought of as merely a children's book. Alice in a dream follows a rabbit down a hole where she encounters some very strange creatures indeed. the Duchess, the Cheshire Cat, the Mad Hatter, the March Hare, the King and Queen of Hearts, and the Mock Turtle. A later book by the same author, *Through the Looking Glass and what Alice found there* (1872) has Alice walking through a mirror, where she finds living chessmen, Tweedledum and Tweedledee, and Humpty Dumpty.

Charles Lutwidge Dodgson (or Lewis Carroll as he called himself as a pseudonym) lectured at Oxford in Mathematics and invented many board games. His books had no moral intention but they do draw attention to some of the more interesting points in life and in logic. The books have many more serious levels of meaning than that of mere children's stories. Take for example the following passage:

'You should say what you mean,' the March Hare went on.
'I do,' Alice hastily replied; 'at least — at least I mean what I say — that's the same thing, you know.'
'Not the same thing a bit,' said the Hatter. 'Why, you might just as well say that "I see what I eat" is the same thing as "I eat what I see"!'
'You might just as well say,' added the March Hare, 'that "I like what I get" is the same thing as "I get what I like"!'
'You might just as well say,' added the Dormouse which seemed to be talking in its sleep, 'that "I breathe when I sleep" is the same thing as "I sleep when I breathe"!'
'It *is* the same thing with you' said the Hatter, and here the conversation dropped, and the party sat silent for a minute.

Lewis Carroll, *Alice's Adventures in Wonderland*

Examine the Hatter's, the March Hare's, and the Dormouse's comparisons with the remark of Alice. *Are* they the same? Grammatically? Logically? In fact? In Mathematics if $A = B$, then $B = A$, but are the English constructions here equivalent to $A = B$? The only verb in English that might correspond to the equals sign in Mathematics is the verb 'to be': *A is B*, therefore *B is A*! Alice and the others don't use this equivalence do they?

Notice, too, how the characters all speak in ways characteristic of the fantastical creatures — the Mad Hatter (hatters were thought to go mad through absorbing mercury used in the finishing of hats into their bloodstream), a March Hare, and a Dormouse.

1. Now select another passage from one of these two books by Lewis Carroll and write a commentary on it about its different meanings and interpretations. (Humpty Dumpty's comments on the meaning of words would be a good one to take, for example.)
2. Invent a short story of your own with three or four animals in it which might appeal on one level to young children but on other levels might have different meanings for grown-ups.

(*b*) Another well-known book of fantasy, full of extraordinary and unreal events and characters is that written by Jonathan Swift, *Gulliver's Travels*, 1726. Most people know of Lemuel Gulliver's trip amongst the little people of Lilliput, where the citizens are only six inches high and everything is in the proportion of an inch to a foot in comparison with normal life. They reflect (on a smaller scale, but in a sense more graphically) the stupid political and religious arguments in Swift's time: should eggs be eaten from the big end or the little end? War almost breaks out on the issue! Should high heels or low heels be worn (with references to high church and low church behaviour in England)? Fewer people know of Gulliver's adventures amongst the giant people in Brobdingnag, his visit to Laputa and its neighbouring continent Lagado where scientists, historians and spectators rule, or to the country of the horses who are endowed with reason (the Houyhnhnms) whose clean society is contrasted with that of the Yahoos, beasts in human shape.

By using different creatures and animals Swift can write about his own society in England; consider the following short passage:

> A fancy would sometimes take a Yahoo, to retire into a corner, to lie down and howl, and groan, and spurn away all that came near him, although he were young and fat, and wanted neither food nor water; nor did the servants imagine what could possibly ail him. And the only remedy they found, was to set him to hard work, after which he could infallibly come to himself...Here I could plainly discover the true seeds of spleen, which only seizes on the lazy, the luxurious, and the rich; who, if they were forced to undergo the same regimen (routine), I could undertake the cure.

What fundamental point is Swift making?

1. Now take three or four things in your own society which you would like to see changed. Use a technique similar to Swift's and write a short story using fantastical creatures to make your points clear. (A reading of George Orwell's *Animal Farm* (1945) will show you another example where pigs reflect the behaviour of humans and thereby show the dangers that some kinds of political system run for us all.)
2. Arrange an 'animal debate' in your English group where each participant plays the role of an animal and represents an attitude or attitudes normally associated with it: e.g. *dogs* = intelligence and loyalty; *ducks* = noise and nonsense; *elephants* = memory; *snakes* = low cunning. Take as the subject of the debate one of the following:
    'humans are not fit to run the world';
    'the law of the jungle is fairest in the end';
    'animals are abused by humans and should revolt';
    'man is an animal like the rest of us'.

Unit 8

Growing-up: youth and crabbed age

*Growing up's wonderful if
you keep your eyes
closed tightly, and
if you manage to grow
take your soul with you,
nobody wants it.*
Brian Patten

This unit is about growing up, through the ages of man and woman. It can be a soul-destroying process unless, as the poet says, you can take your soul with you:

> So,
> playtime's finished with;
> it's time to pull the sad chain
> on his last
> sadschoolgirlcrush.
> It is time to fathom out too many things.
> To learn he's no longer got somebody watching over him,
> he's going to know strange things, learn
> how to lie correctly, how to lay correctly,
> how to cheat and steal in the nicest possible manner.
> He will learn amongst other things, how to enjoy
> his enemies, and how to avoid friendships. If he's
> unlucky
> he will learn how to love and give everything away
> and how eventually, he'll end up with nothing.

Brian Patten

Jacques in Shakespeare's *As You Like It* (II, vii, 142–65) divides life into seven ages and makes each age seem unlovely:

> All the world's a stage,
> And all the men and women merely players:
> They have their exits and entrances;
> And one man in his time plays many parts,
> His acts being seven ages. At first the *infant*,
> Mewling and puking in his nurse's arms.
> Then the whining *schoolboy*, with his satchel
> And shining morning face, creeping like snail
> Unwillingly to school. And then the *lover*,
> Sighing like furnace, with a woeful ballad
> Made to his mistress's eybrow. Then a *soldier*,
> Full of strange oaths, and bearded like the pard,*
> Jealous in honour, sudden and quick in quarrel,
> Seeking the bubble reputation
> Even in the cannon's mouth. And then the *justice*,
> In fair round belly with good capon lin'd,
> With eyes severe and beard of formal cut,
> Full of wise saws and modern instances;
> And so he plays his part. The sixth age shifts
> into the lean and slipper'd *pantaloon*,†
> With spectacles on nose and pouch on side,
> His youthful hose, well sav'd, a world too wide
> For his shrunk shank; and his big manly voice,
> Turning again to childish treble, pipes
> And whistles in his sound. Last scene of all,
> That ends this strange eventful history,
> *Is second childishness and mere oblivion*,
> *Sans teeth, sans eyes, sans taste, sans every thing.*

*Leopard.
†An old, lean fool shown in Italian farces.

In some Greek literature Solon divided man's life into **ten** ages of seven years each. Proclus agreed on seven ages, each one governed by one of the seven planets. The *Mishna* (Jewish 'Oral' law) suggested fourteen ages but the *Midrash* (Hebrew exposition of the Old Testament) suggested seven; Rabbi Ben Ezra (about 1150) divided life into ten stages.

1. Take Shakespeare's division, as it stands, into seven ages: infancy, the schoolboy, the lover, the soldier, the JP, the old man, the helpless dotard. Give to each age some good qualities. (Make a list, if you like, or re-write the verse passage appropriately.)

2. Divide life into the stages you think would be appropriate today. Don't have fewer than five or more than ten. Write down the characteristics of each age as you see them.

Another way of dividing up man's life was used by some medieval dramatists. Instead of dividing life chronologically into periods they showed in plays how man progressed from the cradle to the grave accompanied by virtues and attacked by vices and sins.

The fifteenth-century play *Everyman* is an excellent example of this journey. Death warns him at the start of the play that he'll be coming for Everyman very shortly and Everyman tries to summon up all the help he can. He asks Fellowship (*Friendship*) for aid but once Friendship hears what the journey is about he backs out. Then Everyman seeks help from Kindred and Cousin (*Family*) but Kindred refuses and Cousin finds he has cramp in his toe and can't walk. Goods (*Possessions*) says that he can't help Everyman ('you can't take them with you'!). *Good-Deeds* does try to help and summons up *Knowledge* who offers to go with Everyman to see the holy man *Confession*. Three other characters offer to help him, too — *Strength*, *Discretion* and *Beauty* — but once they take a look at the grave they cry off very quickly. Finally Five Wits (*the five senses*) deserts him, too, and he is left only with Good Deeds and Knowledge to help him when Death comes. Their help allows Everyman to climb back out of the grave and the play ends with a learned doctor pointing out the moral of this play. If your reckoning is not clear when Death comes for you, there is nothing at all that will save you.

The play is a Morality play — a sermon in dramatic form, in fact.

1. Devise with your English group a modern morality play which tracks the course of life from adolescence to death. Have five characters that might help you and five characters hell-bent on the destruction of your soul (e.g. Patience, Generousness, Hard Work, Love, Selflessness; Bad Company, Drugs, Greed, Jealousy, Lust — you will be able to think of others.) Give the outline of the plot and write up the script of the final scene for your English file.
2. Write a short account of how you see your own personal life progressing. What helps you at the moment? What causes you fear and problems? What

will the next few years of your life present you with in the way of help or of
threat do you think?

Tailpiece:

> THE FOUR AGES OF MAN
> He with body waged a fight
> But body won; it walks upright.
>
> Then he struggled with the heart;
> Innocence and peace depart.
>
> Then he struggled with the mind;
> His proud heart he left behind.
>
> Now his wars on God begin;
> At stroke of midnight God shall win.
>
> *W. B. Yeats*

 The notion of God winning at midnight, the hour of death, is one brilliantly set
out by Christopher Marlowe, who lived at the same time as Shakespeare, in his
play *Dr Faustus*. Dr Faustus is a brilliant philosopher and scientist who has sold
his soul to the Devil in exchange for occult powers and knowledge. (Many men
and women sacrifice their lives for one goal or another – – in Marlowe's other
plays it is for money, ambition, political power.) At midnight the Devils come
for his soul:

> Ah, Faustus.
> Now hast thou but one bare hour to live,
> And then thou must be damn'd perpetually!
> Stand still, you ever-moving spheres of heaven,
> That time may cease and midnight never come;
> Fair Nature's eye,* rise, rise again, and make
> Perpetual day; or let this hour be but a
> A year, a month, a week, a natural day,
> That Faustus may repent and save his soul!…
> The stars move still, time runs, the clock will strike,
> The devil will come, and Faustus must be damn'd.
> O, I'll leap up to my God! —Who pulls me down?
> See, see, where Christ's blood streams in the firmament!
> One drop would save my soul, half a drop…
> > (*The clock strikes the half-hour.*)
> Ah, half the hour is past! 'twill all be past anon.
> O God,
> If thou wilt not have mercy on my soul,
> Yet for Christ's sake, whose blood hath ransomed me,
> Impose some end to my incessant pain;
> Let Faustus live in hell a thousand years,
> A hundred thousand, and at last be sav'd.
> O, no end is limited to damned souls…
> No, Faustus, curse thyself, curse Lucifer
> That hath deprived thee of the joys of heaven
> > (*The clock strikes twelve.*)

* The sun.

> I, it strikes, it strikes! Now body turn to air,
> Or Lucifer will bear thee quick to hell!
> (*Thunder and lightning.*)

Enter Devils

1. Learn this passage and present it as a piece of drama with the help of your English group. Perhaps some of you could write and present a modern English equivalent of a scene at the end of a modern man's (or woman's) life, one whose soul has been sold to the Devil for something on earth.
2. Write a modern version of a Faust story from the point of view of the Devil, who has given someone all they wanted in this life and intends to come to claim the person's soul at midnight.

 Growing up through 'the ages of man' is not always full of gloom and doom, however. This section deals with some lighter moments.

(*a*) The first poem shows some of the feelings a parent has during a children's party when the familiar, orderly house is turned over to a strange crowd of young, untamed savages:

CHILDREN'S PARTY

May I join you in the doghouse, Rover?
I wish to retire till the party's over.
Since three o'clock I've done my best
To entertain each tiny guest;
My conscience now I've left behind me,
And if they want me, let them find me.
I blew their bubbles, I sailed their boats,
I kept them from each other's throats.
I told them tales of magic lands,
I took them out to wash their hands.
I sorted their rubbers and tied their laces,
I wiped their noses and dried their faces.
Of similarity there's lots
'Twixt tiny tots and Hottentots.
I've earned repose to heal the ravages
Of these angelic-looking savages...
Shunned are the games a parent proposes;
They prefer to squirt each other with hoses,
Their playmates are their natural foemen
And they like to poke each other's abdomen.
Their joy needs another's woe to cushion it,
Say a puddle, and somebody littler to push in it.
They observe with glee the ballistic results
Of ice-cream with spoons for catapults,
And inform the assembly with tears and glares
That everyone's presents are better than theirs.
Oh, little women and little men,

> Someday I hope to love you again,
> But not till the party's over,
> So give me the key to the doghouse, Rover.

Ogden Nash

1. Describe your own experiences with a group of children you have tried to entertain — your younger brothers and sisters and their friends, an outing, a church toddlers' party, etc.
2. Write an account of the party Ogden Nash describes as if you were one of the children present recalling the event at a later date.

(*b*) The second poem deals with a boy's feelings in trying to come to terms with others who bullied him

MY PARENTS KEPT ME...

> My parents kept me from children who were rough
> Who threw words like stones and who wore torn clothes.
> Their thighs showed through rags. They ran in the street
> And climbed cliffs and stripped by the country streams.
>
> I feared more than tigers their muscles like iron
> Their jerking hands and their knees tight on my arms.
> I feared the salt coarse pointing of those boys
> Who copied my lisp behind me on the road.
>
> They were lithe, they sprang out behind hedges
> Like dogs to bark at my world. They threw mud
> While I looked the other way, pretending to smile.
> I longed to forgive them, but they never smiled.

Stephen Spender

1. Make a list of all the things which bothered you — and still bother you — in your relationships with those of your own age; all have fears and uncertainties of one kind or another. Use the list you make to write an entry in a personal journal — it may take the form of a poem or of an account describing your feelings in prose.
2. Describe a bully or a group of bullies you have come across. How did you deal with the situations they caused? Do you wish you had acted differently towards them?

(*c*) The third passage is from Dylan Thomas's autobiography, *Portrait of The Artist as a Young Dog*, and tells of a game of Cowboys and Indians:

I felt all my young body like an excited animal surrounding me, the torn knees bent, the bumping heart, the long heat, the depth between the legs, the sweat prickling in the hands, the tunnels down to the eardrums, the little balls of dirt between the toes, the eyes in the sockets, the tucked-up voice, the blood racing, the memory around and within flying, jumping, swimming, and waiting to pounce. There, playing Indians in the evening, I was aware of me myself in the exact middle of a living story, and my body was my adventure and my name. I sprang with excitement and scrambled up through the scratching brambles again.

Jack cried; 'I see you! I see you!' He scampered after me. 'Bang! Bang! you're dead!'

But I was young and loud and alive, though I lay down obediently.

'Now you try and kill me,' said Jack. 'Count a hundred.'

I closed one eye, saw him rush and stamp towards the upper field, then tiptoe back and begin to climb a tree, and I counted fifty and ran to the foot of the tree and killed him as he climbed. 'You fall down,' I said.

He refused to fall, so I climbed too, and we clung to the top branches.

1. Relate some of the games you used to play as a child with as much detail as you can.
2. Re-write the account as if Jack were telling the incident rather than Dylan. Decide, before you begin, what kind of man Jack has become so that this can be reflected in the way he tells the story. It is certain that he will be different from Dylan.

Shakespeare's 'seven ages of man' jumped from 'the schoolboy' straight to 'the lover'. He omitted the teenage years with their special difficulties; perhaps teenage problems then were less acute or the teenage years were dominated by 'love' and so ran into that stage. Nevertheless, growing up in the late twentieth century poses problems for the teenager.

Say what the major problems are and set out some of the ways you have set about solving them.

Finding a job is likely to remain one of the more pressing problems of young people — into the 1990s even. What do you learn from the attitude of the young man in the following extract about his relationship with his interviewer?

Youth Careers Officer: Now look, lad. I'm here to help. To serve the public. I'm here to find youths careers. That's why I'm called 'Youth Careers Officer.' I took a course in it. University Sandwich. I was trained in social psychology. I was trained in adolescent problems. So now, button your lip; this is my cubicle. Now, you want a job. What certificates have you got?

Harry: Certificates?

Officer: Mental certificates, lad. Exams. GCE, CSE, DD, Certificates. Qualifications.

Harry: I've got me Bronze Medallion for Life-Saving and me Tenderfoot in the Cubs.

Officer: Is that all?

Harry: Yes.

Officer: So, all we need is a job in a forest, by a lake, saving lives. Did you get anything else?

Harry: No.

Officer: What, did they not give you anything when you left?

Harry: I was supposed to hand me PE kit in, but I kept it.

Officer: And that is the sum total of your academic career?

Harry: Yes.
Officer: Well, we could put you to an apprenticeship on the buildings or in a factory.
Harry: Apprenticeship is no use. Takes you five years to learn what you could pick up in six months.
Officer: You don't want an apprenticeship.
Harry: No, but I want Saturday afternoons off.
Officer: That leaves you with labouring, or semi-skilled.
Harry: I don't want that.
Officer: What sort of thing would you like? Now think about it. I can wait. Take your time. I'm patient. I was trained in psychology and all the rest of it. What sort of job would you like?
Harry: I would like a job with adventure. Like on telly. Lots of thrills. Pioneering, life. Colour. Like the pictures. I was brought up on the pictures.
Officer: Would you like to try the Police? You've got the height.
Harry: I don't like law and order. It usually picks on me. If anything, I would be a cat burglar. But I'm frightened of heights. I keep planning daring daylight robberies but when I get to the stage of shinning up the drainpipe I can't do it.
Officer: Well, all we need to find you is a cat burgling job. Ground floors only. Now come on, come on. I may have done psychology, but I'm not Job. It'll have to be the last stage of a conveyor belt. You can be the human end of a mechanised system. How will that suit you?

Peter Terson, *Zigger Zagger*

1. Rewrite this passage with Harry taking a more constructive attitude to finding a job.
2. The differences in age between the Officer and Harry make some difference to the relationship between them and the language and ideas each uses. Rewrite the passage again, this time with Harry as a young Employment Officer of the DHSS and the older man as an out-of-work, redundant Civil Servant.
3. Compose a job-application folder for a post you would ideally like. This should consist of a covering letter formally applying for a post and a *curriculum vitae* (a 'CV' as it's sometimes known) which gives personal details, academic qualifications, history of your education (with dates), a statement of interests, non-academic achievements you may have, and the names and addresses of two referees. You will find the preparation of such a folder useful for when you leave school, too.

 Old age is a stage in life that many young people find deep sympathy for; many have a close relationship with gran' or grandad, however difficult they may be. Elizabeth Jennings wrote about her relationship with her grandmother and the lasting effect one small incident had on her:

MY GRANDMOTHER

She kept an antique shop — or it kept her.
Among apostle spoons and Bristol glass,
The faded silks, the heavy furniture,
She watched her own reflection in the brass
Salvers and silver bowls, as if to prove
Polish was all, there was no need of love.

And I remember how I once refused
To go out with her, since I was afraid.
It was perhaps a wish not to be used
Like antique objects. Though she never said
That she was hurt, I still could feel the guilt
Of that refusal, guessing how she felt.

Later, too frail to keep a shop, she put
All her best things in one long, narrow room.
The place smelt old, of things too long kept shut,
The smell of absences where shadows come
That can't be polished. There was nothing then
To give her own reflection back.

And when she died I felt no grief at all,
Only the guilt of what I once refused.
I walked into her room among the tall
Sideboards and cupboards — things she never used
But needed: and no finger-marks were there,
Only the new dust falling through the air.

Elizabeth Jennings

1. What was the relationship between the poet and her grandmother according to this poem? Describe it in some detail.
2. Describe your own relationship with one of your grandparents or some other very old person. Mention particularly any times when the relationship has become particularly strained.
3. Write an account of the granddaughter and her own life as the grandmother might have written it at the end of her life.

(*a*) The 'ages of man' have also received attention from painters. In the painting by Breugel *Children's Games*, (signed and dated 1560) in the Vienna Kunsthistorisches Museum reproduced on page 120, the Flemish painter seems to have drawn a picture of childhood, perhaps the first of a series he planned on the ages of man. The picture is full of details of children's games. Some 80 or so have been counted in the picture. The children often look more like adults than children, and some critics have made the point that the seriousness which the children bring to their games is like that which adults bring to their affairs; Breugel was suggesting there was little difference, perhaps?

1. Make a list of as many of the games as you can find in the picture; then describe the games which seem to have been popular in Breugel's day but which have since died out and the games which have survived, with some modifications perhaps into the twentieth century. Add a further account of the picture of village life which the painter presents to his viewers.

2. If you were making a similar painting today, what additional games would you add? Discuss with your English group which of these might survive and then attempt to draw one or two being played in detail, if you wish.
3. Look at the picture at the foot of page 120 and then write a story about it or use it as a basis for an account of your own experience of street games.

(*b*) See the photograph of the artist Renoir (above) in his old age. His hands are twisted by the ravages of arthritis and he was obliged to spend his last six years in a wheelchair. Nevertheless, he continued painting until the end of his life and never needed Shakespeare's 'last age' of man 'sans eyes, sans teeth, sans everything'.

1. Write out some of the thoughts that might have been going through Renoir's head as he sat in his chair, racked by arthritis, thinking of the past and wondering about the future.
2. Visit some old people, with the help of arrangements made by your school, a local church, or some other agency.

   Talk to them about their memories and concentrate on the active things they recall. Then write a report of what you found out.

   Bear in mind, however, that some old people wish to be left alone:

THE GARDEN

Like a skein of loose silk blown against a wall
She walks by the railing of a path
    in Kensington Gardens,
And she is dying piece-meal
    of a sort of emotional anaemia.

And round about there is a rabble
Of the filthy, sturdy, unkillable infants of the very poor.
They shall inherit the earth.

In her is the end of breeding.
Her boredom is exquisite and excessive.
She would like some one to speak to her,
And is almost afraid that I
    will commit that indiscretion.

Ezra Pound

Unit 9

Disasters

If you can meet with Triumph and Disaster
And treat those two imposters just the same
—you'll be a Man, my son!
Rudyard Kipling

The word 'disaster' is derived ultimately from a Latin word for 'a star' (*dis+astrum*). Somehow it is felt that a disaster is beyond our control and lies somewhere in the acts of the gods or an evil force operating in the universe which we can do nothing to influence. Occasionally we speak of a 'man-made disaster', where a human error contributes to a catastrophe.

This unit is concerned with some of these disastrous events on a personal, natural, or universal scale.

1 On Thursday, 9 May 1974 most of the 346 instantly-killed men, women, and children of the Turkish Airlines DC10 disaster in Ermenonville Forest in France were buried. A few bodies had been individually identified and handed to relatives for private burial.

Weather conditions were good on that early spring Sunday morning of 3 March and the pilot taxied briskly to the terminal building at Orly Airport, near Paris. 216 adults and one infant joined an aircraft that was only lightly filled so far. The need to get so many extra passengers aboard, some of whom had not booked in advance, meant that some of the documentation was hasty. It seemed over the next harrowing hours that not all of the passengers had been listed; at least one man was travelling on a passport not his own, and some were using other people's tickets.

The plane re-started its three giant General Electric jets, and taxied along to the take-off runway at a few minutes past noon, carrying 336 passengers and 11 crew. In two minutes the DC10 was off, climbing powerfully into the bright sky, the three engines — one under each wing, a third in the tail — belching vapour and exhaust. The time: 12.30 p.m.

The plane climbed fast on a wide eastern sweep to skirt Paris. Flight plans ordained that when eventually it turned to its north-west course for London it would be at 16,000 feet. Controllers of France's Northern Air Region watched it on their radar screens as it reached a height of 13,000 feet.

And then, quite simply, the plane vanished from all screens.

At 12.35 it crashed into a shallow depression within the Ermenonville Forest north-east of Paris.

On that warm Sunday there were many people strolling along the numerous wooded pathways, but although the aircraft ploughed a thousand-yard furrow through the trees, shearing them off before kinetic energy was expended and the wreckage came to rest, no-one on the ground was hurt.

It happened without any warning. Some claimed to have seen the aircraft explode in the air; others had seen it under apparently perfect control, seeming to make an approach towards some not-too-distant airfield. Others, more expert, had seen it in difficulties at a low altitude, trying to drag its nose up from a shallow dive.

Thirty-five minutes after the crash, rescuers arrived by helicopter. One glance showed there was nothing to be done. Little fires, like those of an Indian village, were separated by hundreds of yards, indicating where parts of the engines and fuel system had ended. Bits of fuselage and human possessions were strewn over the ground; tatters of clothing festooned the branches of trees. No one could have survived for an instant.

How could a plane so fast, so safe and foolproof just plunge to earth on a clear spring day?

The 'black box', which had automatically recorded all the aircraft's movements, was recovered intact, but it merely showed that the plane had reached 13,000 feet and then dived to a lower altitude before crashing. The most popular theory was a bomb aboard but the aircraft authorities were adamant that all passengers and luggage had been screened.

Two years before, in Canada, the faulty latch on a DC10 cargo door had nearly caused a similar tragedy. The door had suddenly opened in flight and this, for a reason which was not at first clear to the crew, seemed to jam a number of the controls. Somehow they nursed it back to base.

Comparison with this 'near-miss' proved that the Paris DC10s cargo door had opened at 13,000 feet. This had caused instant depressurisation of the lower cargo department; when this pressure dropped suddenly the light passenger deck immediately above it collapsed; seats were dragged down into the hold, sucking a number of them in which occupants were still strapped out of the open doorway. The control cables of a DC10, from flight deck to tail, run under the passenger deck and in the doomed aircraft these were instantly and completely jammed. Helpless, the aircraft fell into a shallow dive which no pilot could have righted.

McDonnell-Douglas, after the Canadian incident, made it clear to all its customers that modifications should be made to any DC10 aircraft. The recovered door from the Paris crash showed that a vital flange, part of the safety modification, was missing. For a time a cargo handler at Orly airport was suspected of not having closed the door before take-off but he and the airport authorities were cleared of suspicion.

The World's Worst Disasters of the Twentieth Century

1. Find out as many details as you can of a recent airline disaster (e.g. the Air India crash over the Atlantic with the loss of all aboard or the Manchester fire aboard a plane taking off for Corfu). Write a report, suitable for a newspaper article, on what you discover.

2. Imagine that you were one of the people strolling in the Ermenonville Forest on Sunday 3 March at 12.35 p.m. Using as many details from the passage as you can, describe what you actually saw.

3. Write down what the pilot of the aircraft might have thought and said from the moment he became aware that something was wrong to the moment of impact.

4. On 6 February 1958, the Manchester United team was returning home after a successful European Cup match in Belgrade, Yugoslavia. The plane carrying them is thought to have run into slush on the runway and crashed killing 23 people. Eight star soccer players were killed, including four England internationals. Manchester United had to rebuild its team almost from scratch. Find out what you can about this incident and then write an account of it and its shock effect on the British public, as part of an account of the development of British football intended for publication in a sports magazine.

 Floods appear in many mythologies. A Sumerian tablet dating from *c.* 2000 BC incorporates the story of the Creation and the Flood and there is a Babylonian version of a great flood. Some ancient lists of kings in Mesopotamia divide them into two — those before the Great Flood and those after it. The best-known story about it in the Western world, is, of course, that of Noah in The Bible, *Genesis*, VII.

(*a*) A poem by John Heath-Stubbs gives the story detail and vividness.

THE HISTORY OF THE FLOOD

Bang Bang Bang
Said the nails in the Ark.

It's getting rather dark
Said the nails in the Ark.

For the rain is coming down
Said the nails in the Ark.

Dark and black as sin
Said the nails in the Ark.

So won't you all come in
Said the nails in the Ark.

By only two by two
Said the nails in the Ark.

So they came in two by two,
The elephant, the kangaroo,
And the gnu,
And the tiny little shrew.

Then the birds
Flocked in like winged words:
Two rocket-tailed motmots, two macaws,
Two nuthatches and two
Little bright robins.

And the reptiles: the gila monster, the slow-worm,
The green mamba, the cottonmouth and the alligator—
All squirmed in;
And, after a very lengthy walk,
Two giant Galapagos tortoises.

And the insects in their hierarchies:
A queen ant, a king ant, a queen wasp, a king wasp,
A queen bee, a king bee,
And all the beetles, bugs, and mosquitoes,
Cascaded in like glittering, murmurous jewels.

But the fish had their wish;
For the rain came down,
People began to drown:
The wicked, the rich—
They gasped out pure bubbles of gold,
Which exhalations
Rose to the constellations.

So for forty days and forty nights
They were on the waste of waters
In those cramped quarters.
It was very dark, damp and lonely.
There was nothing to see, but only
The rain which continued to drop.
It did not stop.

So Noah sent forth a Raven. The raven said 'Kark!'
I will not go back to the Ark.
The raven was footloose,
He fed on the bodies of the rich—
Rich with vitamins and goo.
They had become bloated,
And everywhere they floated.

The raven's heart was black.
He did not come back.
It was not a nice thing to do:
Which is why the raven is a token of wrath,
And creaks like a rusty gate
When he crosses your path; and Fate
Will grant you no luck that day:
The raven is fey:
You were meant to have a scare.
Fortunately in England
The raven is rather rare.

Then Noah sent forth a dove.
She did not want to rove.
She longed for her love —
The other turtle dove —
(For her no other dove!).
She brought back a twig from an olive-tree.
There is no more beautiful tree
Anywhere on the earth,
Even when it comes to birth
From six weeks under the sea.

She did not want to rove.
She wanted to take her rest,
And to build herself a nest
All in the olive grove
She wanted to make love.
She thought that was the best.

The dove was not a rover;
So that they knew that the rain was over.
Noah and his wife got out
(They had become rather stout)
And Japhet, Ham and Shem.
(The same could be said of them.)
They looked up at the sky.
The earth was becoming dry.

Then the animals came ashore —
There were more of them than before:
There were two dogs and a litter of puppies;
There were a tom-cat and two tib-cats
And two litters of kittens cats
Do not obey regulations;
And as you might expect
A quantity of rabbits.

God put a rainbow in the sky.
They wondered what it was for.
There had never been a rainbow before.
The rainbow was a sign;
It looked like a neon sign —
Seven colours arched in the skies:
What should it publicise?
They looked up with wondering eyes

It advertises Mercy
Said the nails in the Ark.

Mercy Mercy Mercy
Said the nails in the Ark.

Our God is merciful
Said the nails in the Ark.

Merciful and gracious
Bang Bang Bang Bang.   *John Heath-Stubbs*

1. Where do the moments of humour come in this poem?

2. Which phrases are repeated in the poem? Why does John Heath-Stubbs do this, do you think?

3. Write your own account of the Flood as it might have been seen through the eyes of Noah or Noah's wife.

(b) The same story is treated by a very early English dramatist for performance by shipwrights and fishmongers at York and by other dramatists at Chester, Wakefield, Coventry, and Newcastle well before Shakespeare's lifetime. The most skilled — and the funniest — is the play prepared at Wakefield. There Noah's Wife won't do as she is told and waits until the water is almost round her waist before she makes a final dash for safety into the ark.

Wife: I was never shut up before, as I hope to live,
        In an inn like that!
        In faith, I can't tell
        Which is the back end and which the front!
        Do we have to be shut up,
        Noah, for heaven's sake?

Noah: Woman, listen to reason; here we have to await God's grace
        Therefore, wife, come into this place with a good heart.

Wife: Husband, I'll not turn in for Jack nor Gill
        Till I have done some spinning
        Here on my rock.
        He'd be a lucky man who could touch me!
        Now I'll sit down.
        I advise no man to stop me
        Or he'll get one!

(Noah speaks to her from the Ark)

Noah: Look at the skies! The floodgates
        have all opened — everyone of them!
        Therefore, woman, stop it; get into the ship fast!

Wife: Shut up, Noah. Mind your own business! The better
        for you it will be.

Noah: Now, for the second time, love, come in, for my love's sake.

Wife: Whether I win or lose, to be sure, I don't
        Give a pin for your love! I'll finish off this spindle
        Before I stir a foot.

Noah: By St Peter! I think were talking rubbish.
        Without any more ado,
        Come in if you intend to.

Wife: OK. The water is now so close that I'm sitting in the wet!
        Therefore, I'll get into the ship quickly
        For I'm likely to drown here.

(She rushes into the ship.)

1. Make a dramatised version of the life in the ark *and/or* the time Noah and his wife sight land.

2. Find out what you can about a flood in modern times. There have been huge floods in Florence (1966, when huge quantities of priceless art treasures were lost), and at the Vaiont Dam in Italy (1963, when about 1200 people were swept away and killed when the walls of a reservoir burst with a roar like thunder), and in Japan (1707, 1896, 1960), Hawaii (1869, 1946, 1952), Chile (1960), and Alaska (1964) when underwater earthquakes produced huge waves (known as *tsunamis*) which swept ashore destroying everything in their path. The most well-known *tsunami* was that produced by the eruption of Krakatoa in 1883 in Java and Sumatra.

Write up what you discover in the form of a magazine article. Include some eye-witness accounts from survivors to make your story vivid.

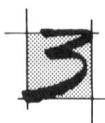 As well as floods, 'natural' disasters come from insects, plagues, avalanches, earthquakes, forest fires, hurricanes and typhoons, volcanoes, droughts, and earth subsidence.

(*a*) In 1985, following a series of television news reports, a huge response to the starving thousands in Ethiopia and Sudan caused by droughts in successive years was orchestrated by Bob Geldoff and pop stars throughout the world. Never before had such a huge international response been made so spontaneously.

Discover what you can about this project with its songs, its concerts, its sale of records, its organised aid with all the planning of shipments, national negotiations, transport, etc., involved. You might wish to assemble a file of newspaper cuttings, tapes, articles, and publicity material which *Live Aid* provoked. Write your own introduction and commentary to the file and include your own original writing in your GCSE English file of work.

(*b*) A natural disaster on a huge scale occurred in AD 79 when the towns of Pompeii, Herculaneum and Stabiae were overwhelmed by a massive eruption of Mount Vesuvius which dominated the landscape down to the sea in Campania. The lava itself reached only the outskirts of Pompeii but the town was covered with successive layers of red-hot ash and other volcanic matter on which soil later formed. The city was, in fact, buried alive. In recent times archaeologists have excavated Pompeii, or much of it at least, and visitors can find paved streets worn away by carriage wheels 2000 years ago, sites of fountains, statues and even Roman houses with their tiled floors and wall paintings intact. Even the town's brothel has survived along with baker's shops and examples of Roman graffiti. On the counter of one shop the charred remains of loaves of bread were unearthed and the bodies of victims, charred and seemingly caught in the showers of hot ash, have been revealed. Not all the town's inhabitants managed to get away in time! It is now as if time has stood still in Pompeii for 2000 years. Not all the roofs are on and there are gaps where houses and wooden structures once stood. Some of the statues are in pieces but it takes little imagination to wander through Pompeii's streets today, to hear the rumble of carts, the cries of traders, and the shouts of children playing in the streets on the sunny day before the town was wiped from the face of the earth. It would be almost twenty centuries before mankind itself would have learnt to extinguish cities like Hiroshima and Nagasaki in such a dramatic fashion.

1. Imagine that you were a citizen of Pompeii who managed to escape at the last minute. Tell of your experiences — moments of immense personal danger and loss, the terror, the screams, the noise, dust, and pain all around you as familiar places crumbled and vanished before your very eyes.
2. Discover what you can about Pompeii before and during its destruction by visiting your local reference library. Begin by looking at encyclopaedias but see if you can discover other more specialised books on the topic: e.g. A. de Franciscis, *Buried Cities: Pompeii and Herculaneum* , Orbis Publishing, 1979; Ian Andrews, *Pompeii*, Cambridge University Press, 1978; Peter Connolly, *Pompeii*, MacDonald Education, 1979.

(*c*) Investigate what steps have been taken to remove or to soften the effects of *one* of the natural disasters listed at the top of this section (**3**). The Thames Flood Barrier, the removal of stretches of water in the French Camargue to reduce mosquitoes, the building of fire barriers in woodland, the inoculation of those at risk from deadly diseases are merely some of the topics which spring to mind. Then write up what you discover.

Discuss with the rest of your English group what they, too, have discovered and use your imaginations to see what more might be done to reduce the worst effects of fateful disasters.

(*a*) Man-made disasters are, of course, preventable in most cases. The biggest of these disasters must be war. It has been estimated that in the 1914–18 war more than 65 million people were involved in the armies of both sides. Of these 8,538,000 were killed and some 21,205,000 were maimed and wounded. It is hard to imagine that there were nearly nine million tragedies of the kind depicted in the photograph on page 131.

The Second World War (1939–1945) was just as horrific, although the numbers of combatants killed and injured were less. However, the systematic genocide in the extermination camps showed 'man's inhumanity to man' as something colder and more terrifying than the heady slaughter of pitched battles. And so the wars have continued — Korea, Vietnam, Nicaragua, Afghanistan, the Falkland Islands...

Read the following poem. How far do you agree or disagree with its thoughts? Do parts of it shock you? Discuss your views in your English group and then write about them in verse or in prose:

UNDIVIDED LOYALTY

Nothing is worth dying for.
Some people would rather
Be dead than red.
But I would simply rather
Not be dead.

I would not die for Britain
Or any land. Why should I?
I only happened to be born there.
Emigré, banished, why should I defend
A land I never chose, that never wanted me?

I might have been born anywhere—
In mid-Pacific or in Ecuador.
I would not die for the world.
Jesus was wrong.
Only nothing is worth dying for.

James Kirkup

(*b*) On pages 133 and 134 are two pictures of destruction, one a train crash and the other the explosive demolition of a building. Use **one** of them as the basis of a piece of creative writing on the subject of 'A man-made disaster'.

(*c*) From time to time horrific fires break out in buildings from which people cannot escape in time before being overwhelmed by smoke. Sometimes the fires are started deliberately and sometimes accidentally. The disaster at Bradford City's football stadium in 1985 was a reminder of how quickly a man-made disaster can strike. A similar tragedy in which forty-six young people were killed and 130 were gravely injured occurred in the small hours of 15 February 1981, at the Stardust nightspot in Dublin where they had been enjoying a St Valentine's Day disco:

It was 2 a.m. and time for the last dance for disco-goers at the Stardust. The club was packed with 841 young people, mostly under 21, enjoying themselves at Dublin's most popular night-spot.

Top prizes in a disco-dance competition had just been carried off by elated winners, the bar was about to close and the disc-jockey was introducing one of the last hit-records that would be played. From the corner of his eye the DJ noticed two club stewards carrying fire extinguishers towards what appeared to be a smouldering curtain. Seconds later the cries of the dying filled the air...

Within moments the entire hall was ablaze. The vast ceiling simply began to melt in the intense heat, raining white-hot droplets into panic-stricken teenagers. The lights went out and youngsters were trampled underfoot in the blind stampede to escape the fireball the Stardust had become.

The inferno had shot out of control so quickly, it is alleged, because the hall was literally a plastic palace. The chairs overlooking the dance floor were covered in red plastic and stuffed with polyurethane foam which gives off a lethal black smoke when alight and can raise temperatures to 1500 degrees Fahrenheit in under a minute. The ceiling was covered in tiles, which seemed to 'explode' according to witnesses. Curtains were draped round the walls and all the tables were made of plywood with plastic tops.

'It was complete pandemonium.' said Eamonn Quinn, 24. 'There were flames everywhere and the whole place seemed to go up in a matter of minutes. The only way out was through the exit doors. The toilet windows were barred because vandals kept breaking the glass.'

D.J. Colin O'Brien witnessed the horror: 'There was just total panic. People grabbed on to me when I was on stage... I ended up behind the stage and was pushed into a ladies' loo. I found there was fresh air there and not much smoke. Eventually smoke came in and I tried to get out through the roof of the loo, but it was made of concrete. I felt my way by the walls until I reached the exit. I couldn't see where I was going.'

Secretary Maureen Ashe, 22, said: 'The noise and screams were awful. I will live with that sound for the rest of my life.' 18-year old Pauline Brady added: 'I saw three girls with their hair ablaze.' Father McMahon dashed into the blazing building to see if he could help those still trapped: 'The ceiling was gone; just the girders were left. There were bodies lying all over the place. The people who were dead were in God's hands immediately. The people who needed help were those outside who were going frantic trying to rescue their sisters or girlfriends.'

On the morning of 15 February, a cold, miserable Sunday, the grim task of identifying the bodies began.

The World's Worst Disasters of the Twentieth Century

1. Write an account of the incident as if you were one of those who managed to escape without injury. Allow your thoughts and feelings at what was happening to merge with the description of the incident.

2. Fire regulations governing places where members of the public meet are very strict. Find out what your local fire-brigade have to say about the subject. Your English group might consider inviting the local fire-prevention officer from the station to visit the school to put his or her views on fire in public places to you and to join in your discussions. A polite letter of invitation, with your headteacher's approval, might well produce results, but prepare in advance very carefully the points you would like to raise.
3. Improvise a dramatic scene where an official inquiry is taking place on the incident described above. Keep the conduct of the business formal and call witnesses to describe what happened.
4. Ask for the fire regulations in operation at your school or college. Do they seem adequate to you? What would you like to see added to (or taken away from) them?

Personal disasters are less spectacular and much more private — but they are more real and more full of pain. The death of a parent, child, husband, wife or close friend; the maiming of someone you love in an accident; the loss of a family pet — all seem events in life, universal as they are in fact, unbearable and impossible to justify.

Here is a poem about such a loss, followed by an explanation of death by the seventeenth-century poet and preacher, John Donne:

DEATH OF A SON
(who died in a mental hospital, aged one)

Something has ceased to come along with me.
Something like a person: something very like one.
And there was no nobility in it
Or anything like that.

Something was there like a one-year-
Old house, dumb as stone. While the near buildings
Sang like birds and laughed
Understanding the pact

They were to have with silence. But he
Neither sang nor laughed. He did not bless silence
Like bread, with words.
He did not forsake silence.

But rather, like a house in mourning
Kept the eye turned to watch the silence while
The other houses like birds
Sang around him.

And the breathing silence neither
Moved nor was still.

I have seen stones: I have seen brick
But this house was made up of neither bricks nor stone
But a house of flesh and blood
With flesh of stone

And bricks for blood. A house
Of stones and blood in breathing silence with the other
Birds singing crazy on its chimneys.
But this was silence,

This was something else, this was
Hearing and speaking though he was a house drawn
Into silence, this was
Something religious in his silence,

Something shining in his quiet,
This was different this was altogether something else:
Though he never spoke, this
Was something to do with death.

And then slowly the eye stopped looking
Inward. The silence rose and became still.
The looked turned to the outer place and stopped,
With the birds shrilling around him.
And as if he could speak

He turned over on his side with this one year
Red as a wound
He turned over as if he could be sorry for this
And out of his eyes two great tears rolled, like stones,
and he died.

Jon Silkin

Death comes equally to us all, and makes
us all equal when it comes. The ashes of an
oak in the chimney are no epitaph of that oak
to tell me how high or how large that was. It
tells me not what flocks it sheltered while it
stood, nor what men it hurt when it fell. The
dust of great persons' graves is speechless too:
it says nothing, it distinguishes nothing. As
soon the dust of a wretch as of a prince will
trouble thine eyes, if the wind blow it thither.
And when a whirlwind hath blown the dust of the
churchyard into the church and the man sweeps
the dust of the church into the churchyard,
who will undertake to sift those dusts again
and to pronounce. 'This is the patrician, this
the yeomanly, this the plebeian bran…

John Donne, *Sermon*

1. Both these extracts are poems and both are sermons, in a way. Can you say which way?

2. What is the main point both these extracts make? Do they differ? How?

3. Write an account of the biggest personal disaster in your life so far.

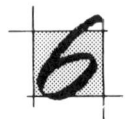

Finally some disasters are treated humorously.

(a)

AN EPITAPH ON A SON

Little Willie from his mirror
   Licked the mercury right off,
Thinking in his childish error,
   It would cure the whooping cough.
At the funeral his mother
   Smartly said to Mrs Brown:
' 'Twas a chilly day for Willie
   When the mercury went down.'

Anon.

(b) Mother and father 'break up':

Mother and father and Mr Lucas had another 'civilised' meeting at about seven o'clock, but when my mother disclosed that she was leaving for Sheffield with Mr Lucas my father became uncivilised and started fighting. Mr Lucas ran into the garden but my father rugby-tackled him by the laurel bush and the fight broke out again. It was quite exciting really. I had a good view from my bedroom window. Mrs O'Leary said, ' 'Tis the child I feel sorry for', and all the people looked up and saw me, so I looked especially sad. I expect the experience will give me a trauma at some stage in the future. I'm all right at the moment, but you never know.

Sue Townsend, *The Secret Diary of Adrian Mole aged 13¾*

1. Write humorously, if you can, about a situation or an incident really or potentially disastrous.

2. Re-write either (or both) of these passages in a serious mood.

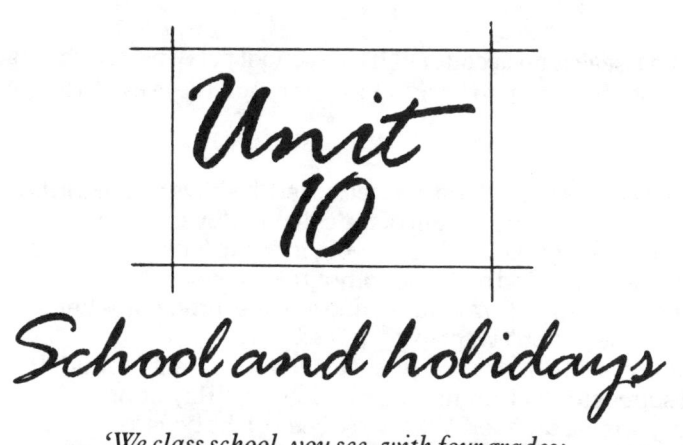

Unit 10

School and holidays

'We class school, you see, with four grades:
Leading School, First-rate School, Good School,
and School.'
'Frankly, said Mr Levy, 'School is pretty bad.'
E. Waugh, *Decline and Fall*

For some, schooldays are the happiest days of their lives; for others they are the worst. This unit is concerned with school seen from various angles — those of the pupil, the teacher, the parent and the outsider.

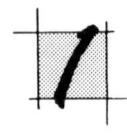

(*a*) The first passage is an account of how a school party passed through the British customs after a trip to Paris — seen through the eyes of a teacher:

Coming sadly back to England, we had asked the boys to make lists of their foreign purchases for the benefit of the customs. 'Everything?' said Samuels. 'Everything,' we said. 'Oh,' said Samuels, trying to look as though most of his purchases were of a kind not to be committed to paper.

'You know, sir,' said Raymond, staring into the turbulent waters of the English Channel, 'I don't want to go home.'

'Oh, surely,' said Charles, 'you want to tell your parents about it.'

'Don't suppose they'll be interested much,' said Raymond.

The customs we dreaded. What we'd seen of the boys' purchases had a generally rather illicit and heavily dutiable appearance. At Newhaven Charles and I hovered nervously behind the party as they produced their lists for inspection.

I've never seen customs officials looking merrier. Those little pieces of paper were passed from one to another, running a gauntlet of laughs. Was it, we wondered, the laughter of officials about to be able to mulct on a gigantic scale?

One or the officers, speechless with mirth, thrust a list into my hand. I glanced at it.

'1 botel shampain,' it said, '100 fags. 1 modle Eyeful Towr. 1 pip. 1 botel sent.'

With an effort I reminded myself that, to an outsider, this commonplace example of Stonehill Street spelling must be comic. I forced a laugh. Charles, peering over my shoulder, did the same.

In their amusement, the customs officers didn't bother to look in Charles's case or mine. Which, as it happened, was lucky.

E. Blishen, *Roaring Boys*

1. Look up the word *mulct* in a dictionary. Why does Blishen choose this word deliberately?
2. Try to describe in detail what makes this account funny.
3. Re-write the description of the incident as one of the customs officials *or* one of the boys might have set it out later.
4. Describe the teacher's emotions carefully that he probably had as the incident proceeded.
5. Describe your own experiences of passing through customs as a member of a school party returning from a trip abroad.

(*b*) A less funny view of pupils is presented in this poem by D. H. Lawrence, who trained as a teacher and taught for two years at an elementary school in Croydon before giving up. The poem may help you to understand why:

LAST LESSON OF THE AFTERNOON

When will the bell ring and end this weariness?
How long have they tugged the leash, and strained apart,
My pack of unruly hounds! I cannot start
Them again on a quarry of knowledge they hate to hunt.
I can haul them and urge them no more.

No longer now can I endure the brunt
Of the books that lie out on the desks; a full threescore
Of several insults of blotted pages, and scrawl
Of slovenly work that they have offered me.
I am sick, and what on earth is the good of it all?
What good to them or me, I cannot see!

   So, shall I take
My last dear fuel of life to heap on my soul
And kindle my will to a flame that shall consume
Their dross of indifference; and take the toll
Of their insults in punishment? — I will not! —

I will not waste my soul and strength for this.
What do I care for all that they do amiss!
What is the point of this teaching of mine, and of this
Learning of theirs? It all goes down the same abyss.

What does it matter to me, if they can write
A description of a dog, or if they can't?
What is the point? To us both, it is all my aunt!
And yet I'm supposed to care, with all my might.

 I do not, and will not; they won't and they don't;
    and that's all!
I shall keep my strength for myself; they can
    keep theirs as well.
Why should we beat our heads against the wall
Of each other? I shall sit and wait for the bell.

                    D. H. Lawrence

1. Describe what makes D. H. Lawrence decide to give up?
2. What was the attitude of the class to their own education?
3. Re-write the incident described in the poem from the point of view of one of
   the class, who is also waiting for the bell.
4. What do you think of the teacher's attitude to his class? Discuss it with your
   English group. Can you understand it?

Once you have tackled the questions based on Edward Blishen's description of a school party returning to England through the British customs, read the following comment on children's spelling in a government report:

> Some years ago a philologist remarked that if one used all possible combinations the word 'scissors' might be spelt in 596,580 different ways. A recent research took a simpler example, the word 'saucer', and examined how 1000 ten year old children tackled it. Fewer than half spelt it correctly, and those who wrote it incorrectly gave 209 alternative spellings. And yet according to the norms of the Schonell word recognition test 71 per cent of eight-year-old children can *read* the word 'saucer' correctly and without any supporting context. This is one of many indications of a fundamental difficulty: that many who have little trouble with reading may still spell uncertainly when they write...
>
> It has been accepted at once that some people will have difficulty with spelling all their lives, but we believe that the teacher can bring about substantial improvement with the majority of children. No doubt the first question to be faced is: does it matter? It is sometimes suggested that spelling is a convention and that if it is of any consequence at all this is slight compared with so many other considerations in the teaching of English. There is no question about its being a convention, but in our view it is a convention that matters.
>
> In the first place confidence in spelling frees the child to write to fulfil his purpose. In the second place spelling disability is an undoubted handicap in society, however many distinguished exceptions may be paraded to refute the view.

HMSO, The Bullock Report

1. Summarise what is the basic difficulty about spelling for many people and what the report's views are about the importance of spelling.
2. How far do you agree with the views on spelling in this passage?
3. Make list of the words you have difficulty in spelling. (Check them in a dictionary.) Can you see anything in the list which shows where your main problem over spelling lies?
4. Bernard Shaw and others have argued that English spelling should be reformed. Find out what you can about their views and describe them. What are your own views about such suggestions?

(*a*) Here is a passage describing a lesson in a school. Use it as a basis for devising a scene with your drama group. (Prepare a script, if you wish, with all the comments you need for directing the action.)

> In the middle of the room sat Gilligan, a very small boy with a most mature chuckle. He was the only one who was quite sure what I meant when one morning in the Christmas term I wrote 'Autobiography' on the board.
>   'It's when a bloke writes his life-story down,' he said.
>   'Man,' I said.

'Well,' said Gilligan. He chuckled. 'Or bloke,' he said.

This, I knew, wasn't going to be an easy subject to commend to them. They had no romantic feelings about their own lives. It is the rare boy with a special twist of mind that likes writing objectively about himself. Johnson the explorer, yes, or Johnson the tracker-down of thieves and smugglers; but not Johnson lamentably twelve years old and shackled by parents and nagging elder sisters.

'Great soldiers and explorers write their own life stories,' I said cunningly. 'But there doesn't seem any reason why we should leave it to them. Even I have had experiences....'

They hooted meaningfully.

'Experiences,' I said hurriedly, 'that weren't perhaps as exciting as climbing Everest...'

'Don't be modest, sir,' said Gilligan.

'Now just let me get on,' I had been tempted, as I always was, to retort. 'I've had experiences,' I insisted, 'that I think could be made to sound interesting.'

'Where was that, sir?' said Blair, his eye suggesting rather than accomplishing a wink. Blair, I'd soon discovered, was the sexually most restive boy in the class. He was always hiding a snigger.

'And you too...' I said.

There was a groan.

'Adventures don't have to be very big to be adventures,' I said.

'Tonsillitis,' said Gilligan cryptically.

'And so this morning I'd like you to write something that could be called "My Autobiography".'

The displeasure was general.

'I haven't done anything, sir,' said Matthews.

'My life's just dull.'

'My mum wouldn't let me do anything interesting, anyway.'

'Blair hid a snigger.

Within five minutes the board was covered with the names of the chief infantile diseases. I marked some books and then walked round the room.

Hutchings's autobiography was a most melancholy document, revolving round the statement that 'Mumps is all I have not had.'

E. Blishen, *Roaring Boys*

1. What, do you gather from this passage, were the major 'experiences' the boys wrote about?
2. How does the teacher try to stimulate the boys to write about themselves?
3. What does he consider are the major obstacles to the boys' wanting to write about themselves?
4. Imagine that you are Gilligan, or Blair, or Hutchings. Write the kind of autobiography he might have written during an English lesson.

(*b*)School seen through the eyes of a young child can be far more terrifying. Richard Church in his autobiography recalled his 'experiences' in Surrey Lane School, Battersea, many decades ago:

> The Headmaster's name was John Burgess, and he was ten feet high. He carried his head flung back, with a grim mouth and chin set against the world. He wore large brown shoes, highly polished and hooded by spats, summer and winter. He flung out these feet at an aggressive angle as he advanced (rather than walked). He was terrifying.
>
> His throne was set at the end of the big hall. In front of his desk, as a kind of altar, stood a long chest, open during school hours to reveal a set of canes of varying thickness and colour, from light switches to heavy cudgels; some straw-blonde, others dour as mahogany as though impregnated with congealed blood. Lying on the array of canes was the Punishment Book, the register of shame.
>
> Boys sent by their class-masters for punishment by Mr Burgess had to stand in the hall, toeing a white line in front of The Desk. To wait there, facing the grim figure or even the empty throne, the open chest of canes within sight, was ample torture, especially if the ordeal were prolonged from a quarter to half an hour.
>
> It broke the nerve of a classmate of mine, when both of us were sent up for persistent talking in school. We had been standing side by side for some time, through a whole session and a playtime, when school was resumed for the last session of the morning and the Head decided to give his attention to us. My legs began to tremble and I felt faintly sick.
>
> The Head moved slowly to the chest and began to inspect the canes, a ritual that he performed with theatrical technique. Finally choosing one, and flinging open the Punishment Book, he turned to the row of urchins.
>
> At that moment the small, inoffensive little boy beside me revolted. He uttered a loud hysterical cry, dashed to the desk, seized the inkpot, and flung it at the awful figure of the Majesty. It burst on that dove-grey waistcoat. For a moment the laws that govern the sun and stars were suspended...

R. Church, Over The Bridge

1. How do you imagine this episode ended? Try to finish it — not necessarily using the style of the writer but maintaining the tension and sense of unutterable threat he has built up.
2. Discuss in your English group what offences you think should be punished in school. What form should the punishment take?
3. There is a marked difference in atmosphere between Blishen's school and Church's. Summarise what some of these differences are and then give your views about them.
4. Take from Church's descriptions some of the words and phrases which show that the writer was interested in using vocabulary to sharpen the details of his picture. Explain in detail how this choice of vocabulary works — by suggesting other words, perhaps, of similar meaning he might have used but which would not have helped him particularly to convey the mood he wanted to his reader.

(*a*) Most sets of school rules are drawn up to tell pupils what they must *not* do, e.g.

Do not run in the corridor.
Do not talk in the library.
Do not arrive late for lessons.
Do not forget the books you need.
Do not disrupt the work of the class.

Draw up a series of ten signs which illustrate some of these 'negative' rules. Usually, but not always, such signs in other activities in life carry a big cross or a heavy bar:

(No smoking)   (No entry)   (No running)

(*b*) Devise a set of ten new rules for your school which are expressed 'positively', saying what members of the school must do. (Try to think of some rules which would help to improve the atmosphere and work and attitude.)

Can you think of any signs to accompany them?

The story which follows is by Isaac Asimov, a science-fiction writer, especially interested in robots and the effects they might have on men and women. Here Asimov uses a setting in 2155 to make a serious comment on the way schools educate boys and girls in the twentieth century. By using a 'time-warp' he makes it clear what some of the strengths and weaknesses are of the system of schools and teaching today.

Margie even wrote about it that night in her diary. On the page headed May 17, 2155, she wrote, 'Today Tommy found a real book!'

It was a very old book. Margie's grandfather once said that when he was a little boy *his* grandfather told him that there was a time when all stories were printed on paper.

They turned the pages, which were yellow and crinkly, and it was awfully funny to read words that stood still instead of moving the way they were supposed to — on a screen, you know. And then, when they turned back to the page before, it had the same words on it that it had had when they read it the first time.

'Gee,' said Tommy, 'what a waste. When you're through the book, you just throw it away, I guess. Our television screen must have had a million books on it and it's good for plenty more. I wouldn't throw *it* away.'

'Same with mine,' said Margie. She was eleven and hadn't seen as many telebooks as Tommy had. He was thirteen.

She said, 'Where did you find it?'

'In my house,' He pointed without looking, because he was busy reading. 'In the attic.'

'What's it about?'

'School,'

Margie was scornful. 'School? What's there to write about school? I hate school.' Margie always hated school, but now she hated it more than ever. The mechanical teacher had been giving her test after test in geography and she had been doing worse and worse until her mother had shaken her head sorrowfully and sent for the County Inspector.

He was a round little man with a red face and a whole box of tools with dials and wires. He smiled at her and gave her an apple, then took the teacher apart. Margie had hoped he wouldn't know how to put it together again, but he knew how to all right and after and after an hour or so, there it was again, large and black and ugly with a big screen on which all the lessons were shown and the questions were asked. That wasn't so bad. The part she hated most was the slot where she had to put homework and test papers. She always had to write them out in a punch code they made her learn when she was six years old, and the mechanical teacher calculated the mark in no time.

The Inspector had smiled after he had finished and patted her head. He said to her mother, 'It's not the little girl's fault, Mrs Jones. I think the geography selector was geared a little too quick. These things happen sometimes. I've slowed it up to an average ten-year level. Actually, the overall pattern of her progress is quite satisfactory.' And he patted Margie's head again.

Margie was disappointed. She had been hoping they would take the teacher away altogether. They had once taken Tommy's teacher away for nearly a month because the history sector had blanked out completely.

So she said to Tommy, 'Why would anyone write about school?'

Tommy looked at her with very superior eyes. 'Because it's not our kind of school, stupid. This is the old kind of school that they had hundreds of years ago.' He added loftily, pronouncing the word carefully, '*Centuries* ago.'

Margie was hurt. 'Well, I don't know what kind of school they had all that time ago.' She read the book over his shoulder for a while, then said, 'Anyway, they had a teacher.'

'Sure they had a teacher, but it wasn't a *regular* teacher. It was a man.'

'A man? How could a man be a teacher?'

'Well, he just told the boys and girls things and gave them homework and asked them questions.'

'A man isn't smart enough.'

'Sure he is. My father knows as much as my teacher.'

'He can't. A man can't know as much as a teacher.'

'He knows almost as much, I betcha.'

Margie wasn't prepared to dispute that. She said, 'I wouldn't want a strange man in my house to teach me.'

Tommy screamed with laughter. 'You don't know much, Margie. The teachers didn't live in the house. They had a special building and all the kids went there.'

'And all the kids learned the same thing?'

'Sure, if they were the same age.'

'But my mother says a teacher has to be adjusted to fit the mind of each boy and girl it teaches and that each kid has to be taught differently.'

'Just the same, they didn't do it that way then. If you don't like it, you don't have to read the book.'

'I didn't say I didn't like it,' Margie said quickly. She wanted to read about those funny schools.

They weren't even half finished when Margie's mother called, 'Margie! School!'

Margie looked. 'Not yet, mamma.'

'Now,' said Mrs Jones. 'And it's probably time for Tommy too,'

Margie said to Tommy, 'Can I read the book some more with you after school?'

'Maybe,' he said, nonchalantly. He walked away whistling, the dusty old book tucked beneath his arm.

Margie went into the school-room. It was right next to her bedroom, and the mechanical teacher was on and waiting for her. It was always on at the same time every day except Saturday and Sunday, because her mother said little girls learned better if they learned regular hours.

The screen was lit up, and it said: 'Today's arithmetic lesson is on the addition of proper fractions. Please insert yesterday's homework in the proper slot.'

Margie did so with a sigh. She was thinking about the old schools they had when her grandfather's grandfather was a little boy. All the kids from the whole neighbourhood came, laughing and shouting in the schoolyard, sitting together in the school-room, going home together at the end of the day. They learned the same things so they could help one another on the homework and talk about it.

And the teachers were people.

The mechanical teacher was flashing on the screen: 'When we add the fractions ½ and ¼—'

Margie was thinking about how the kids must have loved it in the old days. She was thinking about the fun they had.

Isaac Asimov, 'The Fun They Had' from *Earth is Room Enough*

1. Imagine that, with the help of a time-machine, you could move forward to 2155 to meet Margie and Tommy. Write the kind of conversation you might have with them in a face-to-face discussion about your school and their school.
2. Asimov's picture of schools 200 years hence may not be the one you have. Describe how you see schools one or two centuries on. (Don't limit your description to the 'hardware' and 'software' of schools; say something, too, about the relationship between people, attitudes to others' successes and problems, social changes that will have occurred, and so on.)
3. Are schools the best way to educate the young? What other ways of doing it can you think of? (You might like to use this topic as an area of discussion in your English group or prefer to write down your ideas.)

In order to encourage children to work teachers themselves devise a set of incentives and deterrents. Two research workers surveyed some time ago in both primary schools and secondary schools what form these usually took and how effective they were amongst boys and girls:

Incentives (given in the rank order of how often they were applied)

Boys	Rank order	Girls	Rank order
Appreciation	1	Appreciation	1
Good marks for written work	2	Good marks for written work	2
Interest	3	Public praise	3
Public praise	4	Interest	4
Success in test	5	Success in test	5
Class treat	6	Class treat	6
Good marks for team	7	Good marks for team	7
Made Monitor	8	Made monitor	8
Leadership	9	Leadership	9
Good report to parents	10	Good report to parents	10
Material reward	11	Material reward	11

There seems to be only one small difference in the way teachers think they should encourage boys on the one hand and girls on the other. Can you find what it is?

The *effectiveness* of these incentives differed considerably from boys to girls. Can you account for the differences? Discuss this list amongst your English group. The rank orders for **effectiveness** were:

Boys	Rank order	Girls	Rank order
Congenial work (interest)	1	Congenial work (interest)	1
Quiet appreciation	2	Made monitor }	
Public praise }	3	Quiet appreciation }	2
Material reward }		Public praise	4
Good marks for written work	5	Good marks for written work }	
Class treat	6	Favourable report to parents }	5
Made monitor }		Leadership	7
Leadership }	7	Class treat	8
Favourable report to parents }		Material reward	9
Good marks for team	10	Good marks for team	10
Success in test	11	Success in test	11

If this list were made today, how would it differ in your view? You may like to carry out a survey in your school to give your suggestions some basis of fact.

Deterrents were investigated. Here are the deterrents, again in the order in which teachers thought they should be applied:

Boys	Rank order	Girls	Rank order
Urged to make more effort	1	Urged to make more effort	1
Reprimanded	2	Reprimanded	2
Under constant vigilance	3	Under constant vigilance	3
Warned of punishment	4	Warned of punishment	4
Deprived of, or given bad, marks	5	Deprived of, or given bad, marks	5
Isolated	6	Isolated	6
Given detention	7	Given detention	7
Deprived of a privilege or treat	8	Deprived of a privilege or treat	8
Slight corporal punishment	9	Sent to higher authority	9
Sent to a higher authority, More severe corporal punishment	10	Slight corporal punishment	10
		Reported to parents	11
Reported to parents	12	More severe corporal punishment	12

Again, there are some slight differences in the way teachers approached boys and girls. What are they? Are they justified?

This time, try to draw up your own rank order of how effective these deterrents would be today for boys and for girls. Are there any others you would like to add or any you would wish to delete?

1. Now write a report on the behaviour of pupils in your own school and the sanctions that teachers apply to make sure that an atmosphere where sound work and individual development can exist. How would you like to see the system you describe improved?
2. How have attitudes towards discipline changed since the earlier report in 1952? How far do these changes reflect changes in society, too? Have these changes been for the better or the worse? (Too often one hears older people commenting on schools and beginning with the phrase, 'It was not like that in my day…'.)

 Finally, school would not be school without the holidays that go with the work. In recent years a number of organisations, some commercial and some not, have set out to arrange holidays which have the open intention of continuing education and contact with other (but different) groups of children.

On pages 150-151 there is an advertisement for such a holiday. Read it carefully and think about the accompanying pictures. Then set out your ideas that arise from the advertisement. Some questions are given which may help you to concentrate your thoughts:

Holidays for youngsters that parents will heartily approve of

Kids International Day and Residential Camps provide the perfect summer holiday solution for you – and a dream holiday for your children.

From the most energetic 4 year old through to sophisticated young adults of 16, we've a paradise of a holiday in store.

We know that children will simply see our holidays as pure fun – but we offer a lot more than that. Children learn new skills (or perfect existing ones). They use the latest equipment. They benefit from experienced teaching and they make new friends.

The whole of our organisation is dedicated to just one aim – providing your children with the holiday of a lifetime in a safe, caring environment.

If, after reading this brochure, you have any questions, please do not hesitate to ask us – our staff are on hand seven days a week to help you.

A word of warning though – our holidays do go quickly so early reservation is advised.

Kids International. First for choice and value – everytime!

SUPERB FACILITIES

We offer such a huge range of activities that your children will enjoy themselves for the whole of their Kids International or TeenCamp International holiday. And our facilities are truly superb. We've everything from Computers to BMX bikes, Synthesizers to Archery, Sailing boats to Video cameras. Sports of all kinds. And at our Residential Camps, evening disco's, competitions, and a very full social life.

We ask your children to pick five activities as the 'core' around which we build a week's busy programme tailored to individual preferences. (With such a wide choice this could be a difficult decision to make!)

A GOOD MIX OF CHILDREN

Our Residential camps have an international flavour. Children from America, Scandinavia and Europe mix happily with British youngsters. So, appropriately in International Youth Year, your children will come back with a broad outlook on the world, as well as a host of new experiences and friendships.

ALL IN PRICES

With our holidays there are no irritating 'extras' for activity options. Everything is prepaid beforehand: camp T-Shirts, Sports hats, Sports Bags, Coach travel where needed. So all your youngsters need is a small amount of pocket money for their holiday.
Our prices are guaranteed. And you can save money by booking early.

OUTSTANDING SUPERVISION

You can safely entrust your children to us. Our ratio of staff to children at 1:5 is very high.
Many of our supervisors are teachers or post-graduates. We choose them not just for their ability in their specialist subjects, but also for their enthusiasm and skill at relating to young people.
They're fully trained before they get to camp, and they'll supervise your children, closely but unobtrusively, at all times.
So your youngsters can safely enjoy themselves.
(Talking of safety, standards are rigorously adhered to and conform to the guidelines set out by the Department of Education and Science.)

1. At whom is the advertisement mainly directed? What special points are made to make the holiday seem attractive to this audience?
2. What comments can you make about the relationship of the pictures to the text of the advertisement? (Here the pictures have been slightly rearranged since the original advertisement spread over a double-fold in a magazine.)
3. What is there in the advertisement which might make the children react favourably or unfavourably to the suggestion of going on such a holiday?
4. Can you detect any *implied* attitudes or suggestions in the advertisement which are likely to make the holiday seem attractive?
5. What are your views about:
    (*a*) family holidays;
    (*b*) adventure holidays;
    (*c*) leisure/educational organised holidays?

Unit 11

Travellers' tales

The great age of travellers' tales was Shakespeare's, since his age was the age of travelling: in 1577 Sir Francis Drake set out in the *Pelican* (later renamed the *Golden Hind*) to sail around the world; Sir Walter Raleigh went to find gold in Guiana (now Venezuela) in 1595; Richard Hakluyt collected into three volumes in 1598–1600 accounts of the voyages of the Cabots, Sir Hugh Willoughby's voyage to the north east in search of Cathay, Sir John Hawkins's voyages to Guinea and the West Indies, Frobisher's search for the North-West Passage, John Davy's journeys to the Arctic and many more. And all this a century after Christopher Columbus's discovery of America and two centuries after Sir John Mandeville had produced his own book of travellers' tales — a kind of travel guide to Turkey, Tartary, Persia, and Egypt.

Today our travellers leave the world and go into space; ours is the age of the First Men on the Moon.

This unit is concerned primarily not with travels, themselves, interesting though they are, but with the stories that the travellers bring back with them.

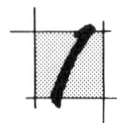

First, two accounts from the Anglo-Saxons and the Vikings.

(*a*) Wulfstan told King Alfred that in Esthonia the king and the nobles drink mare's milk and the poor and the serfs drink mead and there is a big struggle going on between them. And the Esthonians have a custom that when someone dies, he lies uncremated amongst his family and friends for a month — sometimes for two, the kings and other high-ranking men according to the money they have. And all the time that the body lies in the house there is eating and drinking and games until the day that they cremate the body. On that day, the property remaining after all the drinking and the games have been paid for is divided up into five or six — sometimes more. They then lay it out over a mile, the biggest part farthest from the town, then the second, then the third and so on, with the smallest bit nearest the town. Then those with the fastest horses in the land gather five or six miles from the property and then gallop towards it. The one with the fastest horse gets to the first and biggest bit, and so one after the other until everything has been collected up. Then each rides away with the property and can keep it all. For that reason the fastest horses are incredibly dear.

From *Wulfstan's Account to King Alfred of His Voyages*, translated by
R. A. Banks

(*b*) Thorfinn Karlsefni decided to go on a voyage to look for Vinland (the land of wine) in 1007. On his journey he met some small people they called Skraelings; some think these were Eskimos, others that they were Red Indians. In a fight with then Thorwald is shot by a uniped, a one-footer!

The Skraelings had slings, too. Karlsefni and Snorre could see they were setting up on poles huge round-shaped objects, almost as big as a sheep's stomach and black in colour. They flew over the heads of the men and made a terrible noise when they fell. Karlsefni and his men were terrified and they thought only of escaping up river because they thought they were under attack from the Skraelings from all sides. They didn't stop running until they came to some houses and there they had a rough reception. Freydis came out and saw they were running away. 'Why are you fine chaps running away from such worthless creatures?' she called out. I'd have thought you could have slaughtered them like cattle. If I had weapons I could have done better than you. She followed the men into a wood but went rather slowly because she was pregnant. She saw in front of her a dead man, Thorbrand, who had a lump of slate stuck in his head. His sword lay near him and she picked it up and prepared to defend herself. When the Skraelings attacked her she beat the sword on the breastplate of Thorbrand's armour. The Skraelings took fright, turned on their heels and made off to their boats. Later they came across one of the dead with an axe beside him. One of them hacked at a stone with it and broke the axe; it seemed useless to them if it couldn't stand up to a stone and they threw it down.

One morning Karlsefni saw something dash from the clearing; they shouted at it; it was a one-footer and hopped down from where it was to where they were. Thorwald, son of Eric the Red, was sitting at the helm and the one-footer shot an arrow into his small guts. Thorwald drew the arrow out and then said, 'We have been given a good land; look, there is fat in my stomach'. Then the one-footer made off north and they chased it but it evaded them in a bay and Karlsefni decided not to risk their company any more there.

From *Thorfinn's saga*, translated by R. A. Banks

1. Fights with the natives, strange misshapen creatures, and foreign customs form the substance of many of these early (and later) travellers' tales. Creatures with one eye, with heads beneath their shoulders, giants, warrior women, all feature from time to time. Write a fictitious account of an early voyage of discovery yourself, where the travellers meet some very strange creatures.

2. Oddly, many travellers' tales present the story-tellers as the civilised people and those they meet as savages. The same attitude is seen in narratives like Daniel Defoe's *Robinson Crusoe*. Tell a story of this kind from the point of view of the so-called savage! (Many of the Incas, for example, must have felt that the Spaniards in their ruthless search for gold were the savages and not them!)

 Nevertheless, travellers have always been seen by those who stay at home as odd people and the stories they return with are regarded as confirmation that they are wild eccentrics. Even wilder stories are then invented about them to confirm their eccentricity.

(*a*) Margaret Fountaine was one such traveller some fifty years ago. She was a butterfly-hunter and, wearing a pair of plimsolls and a rather large sun helmet, she climbed mountains, tramped through jungles, slept in flea-ridden huts from Damascus to Tibet. Her magnificent collection of 22,000 specimens was bequeathed to the Castle Museum, Norwich, in 1940.

On her expeditions she often wore a man's check shirt with several extra canvas pockets sewn on, a striped cotton skirt with more pockets, cotton gloves with the fingertips cut off, a cork helmet, and plimsolls. Once when going out to India she bought some dresses at Harrods because she had been invited to stay with the Viceroy. The dressmaker was horrified when Miss Fontaine told her to slit open the side seams and insert two large canvas pockets: 'They'll hang all right for the party,' she explained. 'Then I'll fill them with butterfly boxes afterwards.'

She told how she passed a terrible night on the floor of a hut infested with fleas and vermin in order to pursue a beautiful white butterfly later. When she caught malaria in North Africa she began bathing in diluted creosote which turned her a shade of brown. She earned money in America by collecting spider's nests at four dollars a dozen and when she was nearly seventy she rode forty-five miles a day, most of it at a gallop.

Stories of her hunt for men are almost as prodigious as those of her butterfly-hunting. She regularly fell in love with curates and pursued a drunken Irish chorister round Norwich Cathedral in a most unladylike fashion. A baron; Jacques Bellacoscia a Corsican hero who started his career by shooting the mayor of Ajaccio; Dr Popovitch in Budapest; a young Hungarian entomologist by the name of Herr Torok; a twenty-four-year-old Syrian courier Khalil Neimy (already married with two children); an Egyptian ship's officer; and an amorous Brazilian — all received the attention of Miss Fountaine's 'man-net'.

These stories were contained in twelve volumes of her diaries — 3000 pages of vivid prose written in a neat, sloping hand, along with photographs, drawings, postcards, and pressed flowers. Her travels ended in 1940. She collapsed in the heat in Trinidad and a kindly monk, Brother Bruno, found her dying of a heart attack, with her beloved butterfly net just out of reach beside her.

Adapted from M. Nicholas, *The World's Greatest Cranks and Crankpots*

1. Give an account of a (fictitious) eccentric's hunt for adventure in wild parts of the world. Relate some of the adventures he or she meets on the expedition(s).

2. What are your views about the conservation of the world's wild life? Should it be protected from naturalists (even scientific ones) searching for specimens? Take this subject as an area for discussion with your English group or write an essay on the subject for your English file.

(*b*) Traveller's tales sometimes become wild and find themselves immortalised in song:

THE CROCODILE

Now listen you landsmen unto me, to tell you the truth I'm bound,
What happened to me by going to sea, and the wonders that I found;
Shipwrecked I was once off Perouse and cast upon the shore,
So then I did resolve to roam, the country to explore.

    Tomy rit fal lal li bollem tit, tommy rit fal lal li dee!
    Tomy rit fal lal li bollem tit, tommy rit fal lal li dee!

'Twas far I had not scouted out, when close alongside the ocean,
I saw something which at first I thought was all the world in motion;
But steering up close alongside, I found 'twas a crocodile,
And from his nose to the tip of his tail he measured five hundred mile.

  Tomy rit, etc.

When up aloft the wind was high, it blew a gale from the south,
I lost my hold and away did fly right into the crocodile's mouth;
He quickly closed his jaws on me and thought he'd got a victim,
But I ran down his throat, d'ye see, and that's the way I tricked him.

  Tomy rit, etc.

I travelled on for a month or two, till I got into his maw,
Where I found of rum-kegs not a few, and a thousand fat bullocks in store.
Of life I banished all my care, for of grub I was not stinted,
And in this crocodile I lived ten years, and very well contented.

  Tomy rit, etc.

The crocodile being very old, one day, alas, he died;
He was ten long years a-getting cold, he was so long and wide.
His skin was eight mile thick, I'm sure, or very near about,
For I was ten years or more a cutting my way out.

Tomy rit, etc.
And now I've once more got on earth, I've vowed no more to roam;
In a ship that passed I got a berth, and now I'm safe at home.
And if my story you should doubt, should you ever travel the Nile,
It's ten to one you'll find the shell of that wonderful crocodile.

Tomy rit, etc.

Anon.

The traveller's tale of being swallowed alive goes back a long way: Jonah in the
Bible, was swallowed by 'a giant fish' — not a whale — and 'was in the belly of
the fish three days and three nights… and it vomited Jonah upon the dry land';
James Bridie's play, *Jonah and the Whale* (1932), explores the traveller's position
inside the fish:

The Whale: For three days and three nights, out of consideration for your
situation, I have had nothing to drink. Would you mind very, very much if I
shipped a few gallons? Can you swim?
Jonah: You are a sophisticated rhetorician intoxicated with the exuberance
of your own verbosity. Let me out of here. Oh, God, let me out of this!
The Whale: Look out, Jonah!
(*The light goes out. There is a confused roaring sound.*)

1. Produce a dramatised account, even a single scene, of the traveller who had
   been swallowed by a crocodile!
2. Write a poem of your own about being swallowed by a real or imaginary
   creature.
3. Sometimes stories of being swallowed alive are really allegories — stories
   with different levels of meaning. A man or woman can be 'swallowed alive' by
   greed or hate or lust or envy and is forced to live trapped in a dark world.
   Explore this idea of 'allegory' in a traveller's tale you invent about being eaten
   alive.
4. Finally invent some limericks on the same theme. You might begin:
   There was a young lady of Riga
   Who was eaten one day by a tiger…
   or
   There was a young man from Pilaf
   Who was swallowed one day by a giraffe…
   or
   There was a young girl from Gleneal
   Who was consumed one day by an eel…

(*a*) Travellers' tales are full of adventure — and sometimes of romance, too:

In 1984 Robin and Louella Hanbury-Tenison set out on a trek from the Carmargue, through France, to Cornwall on two of the sturdy, white horses of the Camargue, Thibert a six-year-old and Tiki who contracted horse-flu but recovered in time for the start after having been dosed with penicillin and a diet of extra oats.

They had a back-up in the form of a team in a car that would ride ahead of the horses and arrange grazing for them; this team would stay with the horses overnight whilst Robin and Louella rested in an inn. The days were hot and the nights cold and they tried to average thirty miles a day travelling along old brindle paths where they could or along minor roads with all the hazards of cars driven fast wanting to overtake them in a hurry.

From Aigues Mortes, a medieval town, their route passed through the Dordogne to Limousin and Poitiers, down the Loire Valley, across Brittany to Roscoff. There they took the ferry boat to Plymouth.

The attractions of such a journey? The open sky and countryside, a withdrawing from the hectic rush of the twentieth-century world, good companionship, a closeness to the horses, and a return to the simple pleasure of achieving something by one's own efforts. The disadvantages? Well...were there any?

(*b*) About the same time as the Camargue journey, another was taking place away from England:

Simon Winchester set off on a journey across Europe from Oxford to Yalta in the Crimea, in a Rolls Royce 'to try to see and understand those things that both united and divided the multitude of peoples and languages and customs and attitudes...of this ancient and modern continent.'

His journey went from Roscoff in France, through Angers, Tours, and Dijon to Lausanne and Bove in Switzerland. After passing through Zurich he went to Liechtenstein and on to Austria passing through towns such as Salzburg and Vienna. After crossing the Hungarian border he made his way to Budapest where he crossed the Danube and approached the Rumanian border, where the officials were astounded to see a Rolls Royce for the first time in their lives. At the Russian border the car was closely scrutinised before it was allowed to set off for Kiev in the Soviet Union, a city of old 'Orthodox cathedrals, parks and boulevards and queues'. From Kiev, Winchester took a plane to the resort of Yalta in the Crimea before making the long journey home. This was, he said, 'truly, the edge of Asia'.

Winchester certainly discovered a variety of customs, food, clothes, habits, regulations, road conditions, and people. One thing all the European countries had in common, however, seemed to be their sense of the past and their traditions. The Rolls Royce did attract attention wherever it went and hitch-hikers he picked up and customs officials alike were dazled by its opulence and reputation.

Romance? The names of the cities on his route alone map out the historic lands through which he passed with the Austro-Hungarian empire, the Russian Revolution, the Second World War never far away, it seemed.

Certainly Europe is conscious of its past. It is this which those from countries with comparatively little history, such as the United States, find attractive and enviable.

1. Trace the journeys made by the Hanbury-Tenisons on maps of Europe.
2. Which of the two journeys would you have found (*a*) the more attractive, and (*b*) the more challenging? Explain your feelings and opinions.
3. Given the resources you would need, what journey would you like to make once you leave school. Think carefully about *why* you would want to go on such a trip, *what plans* you would need to make, and *what you hope* to discover on it.

 You might like to read an account of another leisurely trek, this time with a donkey through the countryside of late nineteenth-century France. Robert Louis Stevenson recounted his adventures wandering through the Cevennes with Modestine, his faithful donkey friend, in *Travels with a Donkey*, (1879). Stevenson was a great traveller and described too, a canoe tour he made in Belgium and France in *An Inland Voyage*; in 1879 he also set off for California as an emigrant but he returned to the quietness of Bournemouth in 1884! 'For my part,' he said, 'I travel not to go anywhere, but to go. I travel for travel's sake. The great affair is to move.'

 This section of the unit includes some poetry which takes up the ideas and feelings of earlier sections and raises new ideas about travellers and their tales.

(*a*) First a poem about the white horses of the Camargue, the nature reserve of wild, swampy countryside in the south of France. Look, too at the picture of these magnificent horses below. It may raise the question of whether such horses should be taken from their own native habitat, or whether they should be tamed by men and women.

HORSES ON THE CAMARGUE

In the grey wastes of dread
The haunt of shattered gulls where nothing moves
But in a shroud of silence like the dead,
I heard a sudden harmony of hooves,
And, turning, saw afar
A hundred snowy horses unconfined,
The silver runaways of Neptune's car
Racing, spray-curled, like waves before the wind.
Sons of the Mistral*, fleet
As him whose strong gusts they love to flee,
Who shod the flying thunders on their feet
And plumed them with the snortings of the sea;
Theirs is no earthly breed
Who only haunt the verges of the earth
And only on the sea's salt herbage feed—
Surely the great white breakers gave them birth.
For when for years a slave,
A horse of the Camargue, in alien lands,
Should catch some far-off fragrance of the wave
Carried far inland from his native sands,
Many have told the tale
Of how in fury, foaming at the rein,
He hurls his rider; and with lifted tail,
With coal-red eyes and cataracting mane,
Heading his course for home,
Though sixty foreign leagues before him sweep,
Will never rest until he breathes the foam
And hears the native thunder of the deep.
But when the great gusts rise
And lash their anger on these arid coasts,
When the scared gulls career with mournful cries
And whirl across the wastes like driven ghosts:
When hail and fire converge,
The only souls to which they strike no pain,
Are the white-crested fillies of the surge
And the white horses of the windy plain.
Then in their strength and pride
The stallions of the wilderness rejoice;
They feel their Master's† trident in their side,
And high and shrill they answer to his voice.
With white tails smoking free,
Long streaming manes, and arching necks, they show
Their kinship to their sisters of the sea—
And forward hurl their thunderbolts of snow.
Still out of hardship bred,
Spirits of power and beauty and delight
Have ever on such frugal pastures fed
And loved to course with tempests through the night.

Roy Campbell

* The strong, north wind that blows down the Rhone Valley.
† Neptune, the god of the sea.

1. Describe some of the ways Roy Campbell brings out the untamed nature of these wild horses.
2. He frequently compares the horses with the sea. Where does he do this? How does he do it? Why does he do it?
3. What are your views about the domination of men and women over other creatures in nature?
4. Describe some of your own experiences in dealing with horses or other animals whom you love and respect. (You may wish to write down some of your feelings in the form of a poem.)

(*b*) The second poem brings into sharp contrast different attitudes to travel, already referred to on page 155: travel for the sake of getting from one place to another; travel as a release of emotions and imagination. As you read the poem, you might like to decide which of the two travellers you really associate yourself and which of the two you would rather be:

TWO TRAVELLERS

One of us in the compartment stares
Out of his window the whole day long
With attentive mien, as if he knows
There is hid in the journeying scene a song
To recall or compose
From snatches of vision, hints of vanishing airs.
He'll mark the couched hares,
In grass whereover the lapwing reel and twist:
He notes how the shockheaded sunflowers climb
Like boys on the wire by the railway line;
And for him those morning rivers are love-in-a-mist,
And the chimneystacks prayers.

The other is plainly a man of affairs,
A seasoned commuter. His looks assert,
As he opens his briefcase intent on perusing
Facts and figures, he'd never divert
With profitless musing
The longest journey, or notice the dress it wears.

Little he cares
For the coloured drift of his passage; no, not a thing
Values in all that is hurrying past,
Though dimly he senses from first to last
How flaps and waves the smoke of his travelling
At the window-squares.

One is pre-occupied, one just stares,
While the whale-ribbed terminus nears apace
Where passengers all must change, and under
Its arch triumphal quickly disperse.
So you may wonder,

Watching these two whom the train indifferently bears,
What each of them shares
With his fellow-traveller, and which is making the best of it,
And whether this or the other one
Will be justified when the journey's done,
And if either may carry on some reward or regret for it
Whither he fares.

C. Day Lewis

1. The poem is about more than a journey by a train; it is also about the journey through life. Describe the two 'travellers' and their attitudes on this journey through life, the thing the two travellers have in common, perhaps.
2. With which of the two travellers do you associate yourself? Can you describe why?
3. Take *two* comparisons the poet makes. Describe carefully what he is comparing and then judge how effectively he has made the comparison. (Is it justified in every way?)

Finally, in this unit, a look at space travel, space travellers, and space-travellers' stories.

(*a*) Arthur C. Clarke's short story *Expedition to Earth* concludes with a visit to Earth by men from Venus 5000 years from now. Their discoverers find that the Third Planet (Earth) had once been inhabited and they come across an object which they cannot at first understand but then conclude it is a record of life as it was once lived embodying all the values for which Earth civilisation once stood. The story ends as follows:

'It is clear that the Third Planet was inhabited by a number of different species, none of them reptilian. That is a blow to our pride, but the conclusion seems inescapable. The dominant type of life appears to have been a two-armed biped. It walked upright and covered its body with some flexible material, possibly for protection against the cold, since even before the Ice Age the planet was at a much lower temperature than our own world.

'But I will not try your patience any further,' said the Historian. 'You will now see the record of which I have been speaking.'

A brilliant light flashed from the projector. There was a gentle whirring, and on the screen appeared hundreds of strange beings moving jerkily to and fro. The picture expanded to embrace one of the creatures, and the scientists could see that the Historian's description had been correct. The creature possessed two eyes, set rather closely together, but the other facial adornments were a little obscure. There was a large orifice on the lower portion of the head that was continually opening and closing; possibly it had something to do with the creature's breathing.

The scientists watched spellbound as the strange beings became involved in a series of fantastic adventures. There was an incredibly violent conflict with another, slightly different, creature. It seemed certain that they must both be killed — but no; when it was all over neither seemed any the worse.

Then came a furious drive over miles of country in a four-wheeled mechanical device which was capable of extraordinary feats of locomotion. The ride ended in a city packed with other vehicles moving in all directions at breath-taking speeds. No one was surprised to see two of the machines meet head-on, with devastating results.

After that, events became more complicated. It was now quite obvious that it would take many years of research to analyse and understand all that was happening. It was also clear that the record was a work of art, somewhat stylised, rather than an exact reproduction of life as it actually had been on the Third Planet.

Most of the scientists felt themselves completely dazed when the sequence of pictures came to an end…The picture contracted to a circle, centred on the creature's head. The last scene of all was an expanded view of its face, obviously expressing some powerful emotion, but whether it was rage, grief, defiance, resignation or some other feeling could not be guessed.

The picture vanished. For a moment some lettering appeared on the screen; then it was all over…Millions of times in the ages to come those last few words would flash across the screen, and none could ever guess their meaning:
A WALT DISNEY PRODUCTION.

Arthur C. Clarke, Expedition to Earth

1. If you wished to leave a record of the values of our civilisation for travellers from another planet to discover in five thousand years, what would you choose. (Sometimes caskets containing things such as a copy of *The Times*, a set of coins, a pocket calculator are locked up in a lead casket and buried in the walls of a new building for some future generation to discover!)
You may like to treat this topic as a subject for discussion with your English group.

2. Arthur C. Clarke's story is also a satire on the seriousness of scientists, historians, and archaeologists who treat anything from the past as probably authentic and come to some very strange conclusions — often quite wrong. Recently the huge hoax concerning 'The Hitler Diaries' which miraculously turned up left some very eminent scholars with egg on their faces.

Write an account of a true 'discovery' where scientists and others drew some totally false conclusions *or* write a story, in which at some time in the future learned scholars misinterpret something that they discover from our own times.

3. Write a story based on fact or on imagination which is a traveller's story of his or her experiences on a space trip entitled, 'The strangest things I found in space'.

(*b*) Space-travellers' tales of weightlessness provoked some wild responses to the difficulties it caused and the possibilities it offered. James Kirkup in the following poem investigated how it would affect the very ordinary English pastime of taking tea:

TEA IN A SPACE-SHIP

In this world a tablecloth need not be laid
Or any table, but is spread out anywhere
Upon the always equidistant and
Invisible legs of gravity's wild air.

The tea, which never would grow cold,
Gathers itself into a wet and steaming ball,
And hurls its liquid molecules at anybody's head,
Or dances, external bilboquet,*
In and out of suspended cups up -
Ended in the weightless hands
Of chronically nervous jerks
Who yet would never spill a drop
Their mouths agape for passing cakes.

Lumps of sparkling sugar
Sling themselves out of their crystal bowl
With a disordered fountain's
Ornamental stops and starts.
The milk describes a permanent parabola
Girded with satellites of spinning tarts.

The future lives with graciousness.
The hostess finds her problems eased.
For there is honey still for tea
And butter keeps the ceiling greased.

She will provide, of course,
No cake-forks, spoons or knives.
They are so sharp, so dangerously gadabout,
It is regarded as a social misdemeanour
To put them out.

James Kirkup

1. Write your own poem or prose description of how weightlessness in space could affect what are perfectly ordinary activities on earth.
2. Find out what you can about the advantages and disadvantages of weightlessness in space. (Scientists, for example, can now carry out experiments which were impossibly difficult before because of earth's gravity.) Give an account of some of the more unusual things you discover.
3. Devise a short one-act play, full of surprises, in which a group of space-travellers come across the unexpected. Try to keep the plot credible and the action on stage workable — even if it demands a number of special devices and effects.
4. Watch an episode of a television science-fiction series. Then write a critical account of it under the following headings: The Plot; The Characters; The Special Effects; The Dialogue; Its Credibility.

*A toy that bounces about according to the weights it contains.

Unit 12

Sport: past and present

'Well, what sort of sport has Lord had?'
'Oh, the young Sahib shot divinely, But God was
very merciful to the birds.'

Anon.

This unit is concerned with sport. Several pages of every daily newspaper are taken up with the subject, increasingly the behaviour of both players and spectators on and off the field of play is in front of the public's view, and there is a considerable literature on the subject. Quite properly your English file and oral work should take account of this important activity, if you wish.

COTSWOLD GAMES.

In 1636 a collection of poems by Michael Drayton, Ben Jonson, and others, was published. The frontispiece to the book (see above) shows Robert Dover, who had settled in the Cotswolds, acting as a kind of master-of-ceremonies at what became known as the 'Olympic' Games. It also shows a number of the sports that took place at the meetings in the Cotswolds in the early seventeenth century: horse-racing over several miles, hare-coursing, running, jumping, throwing-the-sledge-hammer, pitching-the-bar, wrestling, and quarter-staff fencing. The wrestling involved trying to kick an opponent's legs from under him as the drawing shows, and this feature possibly developed into the shin-kicking contests which featured in later Games. There were also dancing contests to the accompaniment of the bagpipe and the drum and inside the tents set up on the hillside games of skill and chance, such as chess. A mock castle was set up at later celebrations of the Games, from which guns were fired to signal the start of events, just as the firing of a gun marked the start of a performance in some London theatres.

These games were popular and took place at the Whitsun weekend. The start of the Civil War in 1642 stopped the games for a time but they were revived in the Cotwolds probably early in the eighteenth century with wrestling, cudgel-play, and dancing contests for prizes. Later on grinning contests were introduced, where contestants pulled faces through a horse-collar, and donkey races. Cudgel-play developed into 'backswords' contests using single sticks rather than two where a contestant had one hand strapped to his thigh and tried to open up a wound to draw blood from his opponent's head; the contests sometimes lasted an hour or so.

In 1852 the Games on Dover's Hill in the Cotswolds came to a halt until they were celebrated again on 17 May 1951, when the events included shin-kicking, tugs-of-war, boxing, throwing the sheaf, climbing a greasy pole for a leg of mutton, throwing a horse shoe, and bowling for a pig. In 1966 Robert Dover's Games on Dover's Hill in the Cotswolds were revived and are a very popular annual event to this day.*

1. Find out what you can about the early history of a sport you are particularly interested in and prepare a talk on it to give your English group. (Include the script of your talk in your English course-work file.)
2. Discover what you can about the early history of the Olympic Games and other 'Games' in classical times (Isthmian, Nemean and Pythian). Write a brief historical account of what you discover.
3. What games not included in the modern Olympic Games at present would you like to see added in the future. Argue your case in a carefully worded proposition addressed to those responsible for policy in the Olympic Games.
4. Describe in not more than 150 words how to play a board game or a card game in which you are interested. (This exercise needs to be carefully planned; anybody who has struggled to master the rules of a new board game on Christmas Day after a heavy meal will know just how difficult to follow some 'rules' can be. Keep *your* description crystal clear!)

 Blood sports arouse great controversy. Dog-fighting and cock-fighting have long been banned in Britain as cruel and unnecessary. The trapping of animals by means of gin-traps, too, has been banned only after a long campaign by animal-rights workers. Hunting remains socially acceptable for some, although 'hunt saboteurs', as they are sometimes called, continue to protest.

Here are two sensitive pieces of writing about hunting animals; one is in verse about shooting and the other in prose about using traps to kill wildlife:

(*a*)   DAWN SHOOT

        Clouds ran their wet mortar, plastered the daybreak
        Grey. The stones clicked tartly
        If we missed the sleepers but mostly
        Silent we headed up the railway
        Where now the only steam was funnelling from cows
        Ditched on their rumps beyond hedges,
        Cudding, watching, and knowing.

*Details contained in this account are derived from F. Burns, *Heigh for Cotswold! A History of Robert Dover's Olimpick Games*, 1981.

The rails scored a bull's eye into the eye
Of a bridge. A corncrake challenged
Unexpectedly like a hoarse sentry
And a snipe rocketed away on reconnaissance.
Rubber booted, belted, tense as two parachutists,
We climbed the iron gate and dropped
Into the meadow's six acres of broom, gorse, and dew.

A sandy bank, reinforced with coiling roots,
Faced you, two hundred yards from the track.
Snug on our bellies behind a rise of dead whins,
Our ravenous eyes getting used to the greyness,
We settled, soon had the holes under cover.
This was the den they all would be heading for now,
Loping under ferns in dry drains, flashing
Brown orbits across ploughlands and grazing.

The plaster thinned at the skyline, the whitewash
Was bleaching on houses and stables,
The cock would be sounding reveille
In seconds.
And there was one breaking
In from the gap in the corner.

 Donnelly's left hand came up
And came down on my barrel. This one was his.
'For Christ's sake,' I spat, 'Take your time; there'll be more.'
There was the playboy trotting up to the hole
By the ash tree, 'Wild rover no more,'
Said Donnelly and emptied two barrels
And got him. I finished him off.

Another snipe catapulted into the light,
A mare whinnied and shivered her haunches
Up on a hill. The others would not be back
After three shots like that. We dandered off
To the railway; the prices were small at that time
So we did not bother to cut out the tongue.
The ones that slipped back when the all-clear got round
Would be first to examine him.

Seamus Heaney

(*b*) There was the broad porch of an old rabbit-burrow, and the earth stirred in it.
I crept near to see what was alive in that place. I knew very soon, so soon as I
heard a rusty chain chink at its staple. It was the chain of a gin.
   I drew at the chain and brought out the gin. Its jaws had snapped upon the
leg and shoulder of a stoat. The valiant little beast was striving hard for life;
its red back writhed and strained. For a moment its bright eyes looked at me;
you would have said that for a moment it wondered, despairing, if I might be
deliverance from the iron teeth that mangled it. Then it strained and dragged
again upon the wound, stubbornly, without a cry.

I was indeed deliverance. I gave it the mercy of death and left it there lying on its side. But when I turned away the world seemed a cruel place and the sunlight pitiless; the War had come into those pleasant fields.

You will teach me nothing about the stoat and his way of life. I know very well that the little beast is bloody and merciless beyond all other beasts. He is the assassin of the hedgerows. I have seen him with his sharp teeth behind the head of a screaming rabbit. He will come in among the partridge's cheepers and slay them all; he will take Wat, the hare, by his throat. Therefore he may not plead for mercy; indeed, he never asks it; he will die silently when the end comes: this one never cried aloud in the agony of the trap. Yet it went to my heart to kill that beautiful, fierce thing. I would that the foul duty had been laid on another.

Nevertheless, I killed it; it sickened me that I should have to kill a beast that was at my mercy. But I killed the stoat, and I knew that I could not do otherwise.

Oswald Barron (*The Londoner*)

1. Which of these two pieces of writing did you find affected you most? By referring to details in them say why.
2. The second passage is as conscience-stricken as D. H. Lawrence's poem on 'The Snake', which you will find in many anthologies of poetry. How does the uneasiness of the writer communicate itself to the reader?
3. What are your views about hunting wildlife in the countryside? Can you see the force of the arguments of those who would disagree with your views?
4. Attempt your own piece of evocative writing on the subject of 'Hunting', which sets out your own thoughts and feelings and tries to persuade your reader to share them.

Here are a number of sporting headlines from recent years. Take one and write the article that might have accompanied it.

(a)
'You can't be serious, man'
Tennis star attacks unsmiling umpire.

(b)
'England's batsmen bowled over!

(c)
Eleven-year-old Checkmates Grand Master

(d)

Cramp robs star of record at the line

(e)

Horse-trial course-designer's 'Impossible' fence

(f) **Boat-race sunk**

(g)

'Speedway track waterlogged after cloudburst

(h)

Goalpost snaps as team cracks

(i)

Wrestler says 'I was big when I was small!'

Here is an account of a horrific incident in a Brussels football stadium at a European Cup Final match between Liverpool and Juventus in May 1985. It came after years of growing violence and hooliganism in British stadiums which caused Europeans to re-think the phrase 'le fair-play' which they had borrowed from the English:

41 soccer fans die in stampede at Euro Cup final

From David Miller, Brussels

At least 41 soccer fans died and more then 150 were seriously injured when a 6ft concrete wall topped with fencing collapsed at the front of terracing 45 minutes before the scheduled start of last night's European Cup final in Brussels between Liverpool and Juventus of Turin.

Brussels police said last night no Britons were believed killed. The Belgian soccer federation said 25 of the dead were Italian, seven Belgian, one French and eight remained unidentified.

The start of the match was delayed as officials and ambulancemen cleared the terraces, and finally kicked off 83 minutes late in front of a crowd of 58,000.

After the game had been lost 1-0, Joe Fagan, the Liverpool manager, said: "We obviously knew there were problems, but we didn't know about the deaths".

Mr Charles Ferdinand Nothomb, the Belgian Interior Minister said last night on BBC Newsnight that the cause was that among the British supporters there were so many who wanted violence.

"We took more precautions than for any other football match of this importance because we feared violence from the British, but we had no idea it would be so brutal. I would be very cautious before letting such people come here again."

Uefa officials early this morning said that an immediate private inquiry would be held.

The disaster occurred when the wall at one end of the stadium gave way during a stampede by Italian spectators after they were charged by a section of the Liverpool crowd.

There could be little doubt that Liverpool supporters were primarily responsible, and it must be expected that British clubs will be banned from European football.

The scenes in one corner of the stadium were of pandemonium, as helmeted Red Cross and emergency hospital services tried to cope with the injured in the middle of a stampede that continued even after it was evident that some were dead.

Emergency surgical tents were set up by the Belgian Army in the car park in front of the main stand of the Olympic Stadium.

At least 20 dead bodies when I was able to get near to the scene were covered with tarpaulin as nurses stepped among the injured, trying to determine those who were still alive and to give them transfusions, artificial respiration and other emergency life support.

With bodies still on the terraces among a pile of clothes and debris, the estimated number of dead was increasing every 15 minutes.

The wail of ambulance sirens ferrying the injured to hospital was never-ending and in the pandemonium there were dozens of unattended injured, sobbing and being comforted by friends and relatives.

The suddenness of the incident made it impossible for the emergency services immediately to cope.

It is thought that most of the dead and injured were Italians, for it was their section of the terraces at one end where the barriers collapsed. But it has to be said that the security arrangements were woefully inadequate.

There was an empty area between the rival supporters. But with 45 minutes to go to kick-off Liverpool supporters broke the inadequate barriers separating them from the Italians, who had been incensed by a hail of rockets and missiles from the Liverpool section.

The Italians panicked, turned and rushed towards the one main exit in that corner. Dozens were trampled underfoot or crushed against barriers.

Hundreds of Italian supporters escaped on to the pitch, and other fights around the stadium broke out between rival fans and with the police, who sent in platoons of men armed with helmets and shields.

After almost an hour the pitch had still not properly been cleared while, unknown to most of the crowd, the dead and injured were still being carried from the terraces, some of them on torn-out barriers.

At one stage Joe Fagan, the Liverpool manager who had announced his retirement earlier in the day, wept as he went out on to the pitch in a red Liverpool shirt to try instil some order.

"This is a football match," he told the crowd. "It is my last game as manager, and you are spoiling it. Get back and be sensible." The sta-

dium followed with broadcast appeals in English, Italian, French and Dutch.

But by then it was too late. The fighting had become fragmented and isolated in small groups.

Nobody, of whatever nationality, could attempt to defend England's wretched record of crowd misbehaviour, but it must be said that the Heysel Stadium, in which Sebastian Coe ran the world mile record in 1981, was ill-equipped both in its structure and in the segregation of rival supporters to cope with a match in which there were bound to be such tensions.

It was quite disgraceful, for instance, that 75 minutes after scheduled kick-off time a group of Italians were allowed to advance across the running track carrying a 30ft banner proclaiming "Reds animals". They kept it aloft for some minutes without any action from the police.

Immediately after the display of this banner, the two captains came to the public address system to appeal to the crowd. Phil Neal of Liverpool said: "We are sick and tired of waiting in the dressing room; we want to perform for you. Let's have some common sense and a lot of order and let's get on with it."

There was then an appeal by Caetano Scirea of Juventus to the Italian crowd. Both received cheers at the respective ends, but a small group of Italians were still fighting riot police across the running track.

Hundreds of riot police eventually had the whole stadium under control, it seemed.

The majority of Liverpool

supporters, who in four previous European finals have been involved in comparatively little trouble, were again well behaved. One of the reasons why they burst into the empty, so-called safety area separating them from the Italians was that they themselves were undoubtedly too tightly packed. Aggression was only part of the factor.

Again drink was a major factor, for thousands of the Italians and Merseysiders had been in the bars around town for hours beforehand.

An hour before the kick-off, within a few hundred yards of the stadium, I saw Liverpool supporters drinking themselves insensible, with a pint in each hand, and urinating within the bars where they were drinking.

There was the usual intolerable element of taunting between rivals with their garish flags and banners, an invitation to disorder.

The banners draped on the front railings included many obscene taunts not at Juventus but at English rivals Manchester United, the FA Cup winners, and against the Manchester manager, Ron Atkinson.

By the end of the game police had drafted in massive extra support, with rows of police vans army trucks and medical teams. Groups of rival fans were led through lines of riot police and herded into fleets of coaches and trams.

Belgian radio appealed to residents not to go out during the night and particularly advised people to stay away from the railway station areas.

The Brussels fire chief, Mr Van Compel, said: "Your

British football fans are murderers – and you can quote me."

●A Brussels fire chief said: "It's like a war scene". Most of the casualties came when a 6ft concrete wall topped with fencing collapsed (PA reports).

Mr John Welsh, aged 27, from Toxteth, was in the middle of the appalling scenes.

He said: "The wall collapsed and people were trapped by rubble and dead bodies. It was terrible. Nobody seemed to be doing anything. One man thought his 14-year-old daughter had been killed."

Mr Welsh said: "We were trying to pull out, but idiots were still pushing. I've finished with Liverpool until those idiot supporters go away."

Mr René Buitenkant, from Holland, said: "I saw a little boy about six or seven injured. His father was dying at his feet."

He added: "Liverpool and Juventus fans were playing football together outside the stadium, but once inside they turned to animals. The vast majority of those of those involved were completely drunk."

●British supporters were involved in several incidents, including a jewellery raid, hours before the final was due (AFP report).

The emergency number to ring for details of the injured in Brussels is 010 322 5179611

The Times, 30 May 1985

1. Give an account of the incident based on this report as it might have been given by a Belgian father who witnessed it after he had entered the stadium with his young son and daughter to enjoy a football match.
2. What are your views about violence and hooliganism in sports stadiums. What causes it? What can be done to eliminate it?

 The following are some sporting accounts from the diary of Samuel Pepys, written in the middle of the seventeenth century. They provide interesting evidence of the Englishman's keen interest in sport:

August 10, 1660
After dinner I went by water to Whitehall to the Privy Seal, and that done with Mr Moore and Creed to Hide Park by coach, and saw a fine foot-race three times round the Park between an Irishman and Crow, that was once my Lord Claypoole's footman. Crow beat the other by above two miles.

May 15, 1663
Up betimes and walked to St James's, where Mr Coventry being in bed I walked in the Park, discoursing with the keeper of Pell Mell*, who was sweeping it; who told me of what the earth is mixed that do floor the Mall, and that over all there is cockle-shells powdered and spread to keep it fast; which however in dry weather turns to dust and deads the ball.

May 27, 1663
This day there was a great thronging to Banstead Downs, upon a great horse-race and foot-race. I am sorry I could not go thither.

*Pall Mall was so-called because of the game played along it. A boxwood ball was driven through an iron ring which was suspended at some height above the ground in a long alley; the player who, starting from one end, could drive the ball through the ring with the fewest strokes won the game. (Explanation from O. F. Morshead, *Everybody's Pepys*, 1926.)

December 21, 1663

I did go to Shoe Lane to see a cocke-fighting at a new pit there, a sport I was never at in my life; but, Lord! to see the strange variety of people, from Parliament-man to the poorest 'prentices, bakers, brewers, butchers, draymen, and what not; and all these fellows one with another in swearing, cursing and betting. I soon had enough of it, and yet I would not have seen it but once, it being strange to observe the nature of these poor creatures, how they will fight till they drop down dead upon the table, and strike after they are ready to give up the ghost, not offering to run away when they are weary or wounded past doing further; whereas where a dunghill brood comes he will, after a sharp stroke that pricks him, run off the stage, and then they wring off his neck without more ado, whereas the other they preserve, though their eyes be both out, or breed only of a true cock of the game. The rule is if any man will bet £10 to a crowne, and nobody take the bet, the game is given over and not sooner. One thing more it is strange to see how people of this poor rank, that look as if they had not bread to put in their mouths, shall bet three or four pounds at one bet and lose it, and yet bet as much the next battle (so they call every match of two cocks); so that one of them will lose £10 or £20 at a meeting.

December 26, 1664

So home to bed, where my people and wife innocently play at cards very merry, and I to bed, leaving them to their sport and blindman's buff.

Samuel Pepys, *Diary*

(Other games mentioned by Pepys include sliding with skates, prize-fights, wrestling, bowls, nine-pins, tennis, and shuffleboard.)

1. Write a diary of your own to cover the major sporting events you have seen either 'live' or on television and which is intended to provide a record of your impressions for a reader some 300 years hence.
2. Write an account of two very unusual and minority games that you know of but which will interest a wider audience. (e.g. Eton or Rugby fives; a dictionary of sports and games will help — but don't merely copy out the entries you find there!)
3. Imagine that you were a competitor or a spectator at one of the sporting events Pepys described. Give your own account of it, bearing in mind the noise, the audience, the setting, and the spectacle.

Sport is usually taken very seriously by the British. Occasionally poets and writers see the ridiculousness of some of it:

(*a*)

RUGBY LEAGUE GAME

Sport is absurd, and sad.
Those grown men, just look,
In those dreary long blue shorts,
Those ringed stockings, Edwardian,
Balding pates, and huge
Fat knees that ought to be heroes'.

Grappling, hooking, gallantly tackling —
Is all this courage really necessary? —
Taking their good clean fun
So solemnly, they run each other down
With earnest keenness, for the honour of
Virility, the cap, the county side.

Like great boys they roll each other
In the mud of public Saturdays,
Groping their blind way back
To noble youth, away from the bank,
The wife, the pram, the spin drier,
Back to the spartan freedom of the field.

Back, back to the days when boys
Were men, still hopeful, and untamed.
That was then: a gay
And golden age ago.
Now, in vain, domesticated,
Men try to be boys again.

James Kirkup

1. Write your own account of sport beginning, 'Sport is absurd, and sad...'
2. Discuss with your English group one of the following topics:
    (*i*)   Sport is an over-rated pastime.
    (*ii*) National sports reflect the national character.
    (*iii*) Sport is the surest way of creating a healthy mind in a healthy body.

APPENDIX 1

Keys to objective tests

(a) Unit One: G. Greene, *The Case for the Defence*
     1,A; *2*,B; *3*,A; *4*,D; *5*,E; *6*,D; *7*,B; *8*,A; *9*,A; *10*,C; *11*,B; *12*,A; *13*,E; *14*,B; *15*,D; *16*,E; *17*,C; *18*,D; *19*,A; *20*,C.

(a) Unit Five: Bob Houlton 'My Apprenticeship', *The Listener*
     1,C; *2*,D; *3*,C; *4*,E; *5*,D; *6*,A; *7*,E; *8*,C; *9*,B; *10*,A; *11*,B; *12*,B; *13*,C; *14*,E; *15*,D; *16*,E; *17*,D; *18*,B; *19*,B; *20*,A.

ISBN 0-340-38991-5

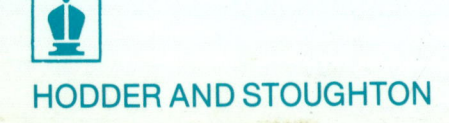
HODDER AND STOUGHTON